The Chambers Family in Philadelphia

Descended from

George Chambers

Born c 1815 in Ireland

The Chambers Family in Philadelphia

Descended from

George Chambers

Born c 1815 in Ireland

Kathryn Chambers Torpey
Alexandria, Virginia

Kathryn Chambers Torpey is a professional genealogist and researcher. She is certified by the Board for Certification of Genealogists℠.

Other Books by Kathryn Chambers Torpey:

John Kennedy of County Donegal, Ulster, Ireland, and His Descendants - A Compiled Genealogy (Including Risk, McCoy, and Pendleton), 2006

William Kennedy of Chester County, Pennsylvania, and His Descendants - A Compiled Genealogy (Including Davis, Smith, Wallace, Russell, and McClure), 2014

Colonial and Revolutionary Kennedy Families from Southeastern Pennsylvania, 2015

The Edwards/Scott Family History - Edinburgh to Philadelphia, 2016

Imprint: CreateSpace Independent Publishing Platform

ISBN-13: 978-1540463838
ISBN-10: 1540463834

Torpey Books
5035 Domain Place
Alexandria, VA
22311-5066

In Memory of my father,
William Scott Chambers

Contents

INTRODUCTION

This family history documents the life of George and Elizabeth Chambers; their three children, George Washington, William, and Emma; and their seven grandchildren who were the children of George Washington Chambers.

The first part of the narrative describes what little is known about the arrival of George and Elizabeth Chambers in America and the early history of the Chambers family in Philadelphia. The second part of the narrative documents what is known about George Washington Chambers' service in the Civil War, his work as a boatman, and his married life. The third part of the narrative profiles the life of each of George Washington Chambers' children - first the girls and then the boys.

The purpose of the document is to chronicle the sequence of major events in the life of the Chambers family; to bring the family back to life, albeit only momentarily; and to depict their fundamental character and outlook on life as a working class family living in Philadelphia during the period 1840 to 1940.

The research for this family history was conducted in three general time frames. The first family tree was compiled by my father, William Scott Chambers, in the 1950s. It was based on oral tradition in the Chambers family which stated that George Washington Chambers was born in Philadelphia on February 22, 1841. Nothing more was done to document the Chambers family history until about 1985 when my mother, Gloria Freda Chambers, wrote a letter to the National Archives in Washington, D.C., requesting a copy of George Washington Chambers' Civil War pension file. The documents in the file, including sworn depositions, provided more complete information about George Washington Chambers, his wife, Annie Edwards Chambers, and their children, but nothing about his parents or the origins of the Chambers family in Ireland.

The balance of the original research contained in this family history was conducted between 1995 and 2000 in Washington, D.C., at the National Archives, the Library of Congress, the National Genealogical Society Library, and the Daughters of the American Revolution Library. Substantial research was also conducted at the Latter-Day Saints Family History Center located in McLean, Virginia. Site visits were made to the Free Library of Philadelphia, the Philadelphia City Archives, the Genealogical Society of Pennsylvania, and the Historical Society of Pennsylvania all located in Philadelphia and to Arlington Cemetery located in Drexel Hill, Pennsylvania, Old Cathedral Cemetery and Mount Moriah Cemetery both located in Philadelphia, Pennsylvania, and to Locustwood Cemetery located in Cherry Hill, New Jersey.

Extensive interviews were conducted with William Scott Chambers and Josephine Thompson Marshall, first cousins who descend from George Washington Chambers' oldest son, William Scott Chambers and, to a lesser extent, with Cynthia Scott Chambers, David Harrington Marshall, Jr., and Jo-Ann Chambers Smith Skinner, three of the great-great grandchildren of George Washington Chambers. During the course of this research, contact was also reestablished with the descendants of George Washington Chambers' youngest son, George

Edwards Chambers, after a hiatus of over fifty years. Providing their recollections of the Chambers family history from their perspective were George Richards Chambers, Jr., Dorothy Chambers Brooks, and Joseph D. Chambers, siblings, all of whom are great-grandchildren of George Washington Chambers.

In conjunction with the preparation of this family history, a great deal of correspondence was carried out with numerous institutions and facilities including the following: Mount Moriah Cemetery, the Catholic Cemeteries Office, the Oliver Bair Funeral Home, the Garzone Funeral Home, and the Historical Society of the Eastern Pennsylvania Conference of the United Methodist Church all of which are located in Philadelphia; Arlington Cemetery in Drexel Hill, Pennsylvania; the Philadelphia Archdiocesan Historical Research Center in Wynnewood, Pennsylvania; the Pennsylvania Vital Statistics Office in New Castle, Pennsylvania; the Railroad Retirement Board in Chicago, Illinois; the United Transportation Union (formerly known as the Brotherhood of Locomotive Firemen and Enginemen) in Cleveland, Ohio; the National Personnel Records Center in St. Louis, Missouri; the National Maritime Center in Arlington, Virginia; the Division of Vital Records in Richmond, Virginia; the Russian Embassy in Washington, D.C.; the Historical Society of Cecil County in Elkton, Maryland; the Camden County Historical Society in Camden, New Jersey; Locustwood Cemetery in Cherry Hill, New Jersey; the Masonic Home of New Jersey in Burlington, New Jersey; the Eastern Star Grand Chapter in Bridgewater, New Jersey; the Historical Society of Princeton and the Princeton Public Library in Princeton, New Jersey; the Delaware Public Archives in Dover, Delaware; and the Connecticut Vital Statistics Office in Hartford, Connecticut. A professional researcher, Susan Koelble of Bareroots Research Services in Southampton, Pennsylvania, was also engaged to review probate files and deed books in Philadelphia with respect to the unsuccessful effort to locate the descendants of George Washington Chambers' daughter, Emma (Chambers) Spence.

Also included in this family history is a 4-generation pedigree chart (at Appendix A) and an oral history of the Chambers family prepared from the recollections of my father, William Scott Chambers (at Appendix B). It documents the history of his branch of the Chambers family from roughly 1916 to 1992. In conjunction with the preparation of the oral history, my husband, M. Joseph Torpey, and I took an 11-day trip to Cuba in June 2000 with a small group of students from Northern Virginia Community College. During that trip, my husband and I made three visits to Dellis Gray, my family's former housekeeper. During these visits, Dellis and I spent the majority of our time reminiscing about life in Cuba, her family history, and what we both have been doing since we last saw each other in March 1960. After our return from the trip, my conversations with Dellis Gray were supplemented by the recollections of Estela Gonzalez Barry whose mother, Daisy Ricketts Gonzalez, knew our family when we lived in Cuba.

The prior research was re-reviewed and updated in 2016 in anticipation of publication of this volume. During that time, significant progress was made locating additional documentation concerning George and Elizabeth Chambers and their son, William, and their daughter, Emma (Chambers) Clark and her family.

Kathryn C. Torpey
November 15, 2016

Descendant Chart
for George and Elizabeth Chambers

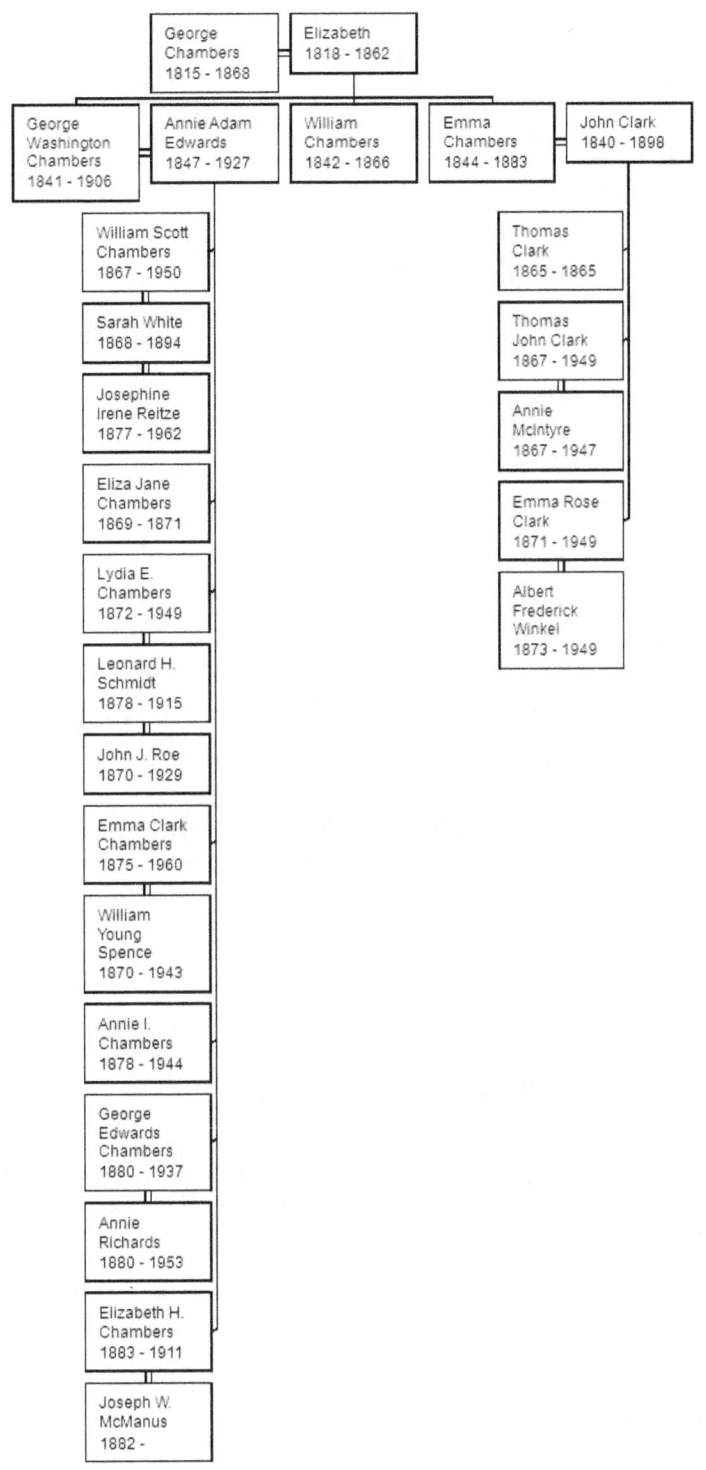

| George Chambers 1815 - 1868 | Elizabeth 1818 - 1862 |

George Washington Chambers 1841 - 1906 | Annie Adam Edwards 1847 - 1927 | William Chambers 1842 - 1866 | Emma Chambers 1844 - 1883 | John Clark 1840 - 1898

William Scott Chambers 1867 - 1950

Sarah White 1868 - 1894

Josephine Irene Reitze 1877 - 1962

Eliza Jane Chambers 1869 - 1871

Lydia E. Chambers 1872 - 1949

Leonard H. Schmidt 1878 - 1915

John J. Roe 1870 - 1929

Emma Clark Chambers 1875 - 1960

William Young Spence 1870 - 1943

Annie I. Chambers 1878 - 1944

George Edwards Chambers 1880 - 1937

Annie Richards 1880 - 1953

Elizabeth H. Chambers 1883 - 1911

Joseph W. McManus 1882 -

Thomas Clark 1865 - 1865

Thomas John Clark 1867 - 1949

Annie McIntyre 1867 - 1947

Emma Rose Clark 1871 - 1949

Albert Frederick Winkel 1873 - 1949

The Chambers Family History

The townland of origin of the Chambers family is unknown. So is their religious affiliation. They came to America as part of the pre-famine exodus of Ireland which took place from 1815 to 1844. The exodus was dominated by Irish Protestants who generally regarded emigration not as exile, but as an opportunity or, at worst, an escape to a better place. Typically, as Irish Protestants became more upwardly mobile, they began to see emigration in positive, secular, and individualistic terms. They rarely blamed the British government for their need to go abroad but instead left Ireland willingly carrying their talent, industry, and energy with them to a distant and happier land. They seldom thought about the land they left behind.[1]

IMMIGRATION TO AMERICA

George and Elizabeth Chambers were our Irish Protestant pre-famine immigrant ancestors. As best can be determined, they entered the United States on September 30, 1840, at Eastport, Maine, through the Passamaquoddy Customs District. They were traveling in the company of a younger family member named William Chambers.[2,3]

Cross-Channel Passage

Their port of embarkation from Ireland is unknown, but they probably sailed first to Liverpool (or possibly Greenock, Scotland) in a trip fraught with perils and inconveniences.[4] By all accounts, their cross-channel passage from Ireland to Liverpool was probably a miserable trip lasting anywhere from 14 to 30 hours. During their trip George and Elizabeth Chambers would have been packed shoulder-to-shoulder on an open deck where accidents were common, there were no safety precautions, and, during heavy seas, they would have held onto each other to avoid being washed overboard while being drenched with cold seawater and awash in their own vomit. Upon arrival in Liverpool, there would have been no safe haven for them. Instead, they

---

[1]Kerby A. Miller, *Emigrants and Exiles - Ireland and the Irish Exodus to North America*, (New York: Oxford University Press, 1985), 228.

[2]A Supplemental Index to Passenger Lists of Vessels Arriving at Atlantic and Gulf Ports (Excluding New York), 1820-1874, National Archives Microfilm Publication M334, Roll 27. Note: The index includes cards for George Chambers (25), Elizabeth Chambers (22), and William Chambers (20) all of whom were traveling together from Ireland to the United States. The two men were listed as laborers.

[3]Lists of Passengers Arriving at Miscellaneous Ports on the Atlantic and Gulf Coasts and Ports on the Great Lakes, 1820-1873, National Archives Microfilm Publication M575, Roll 7. Note: The passenger lists for the Third Quarter of 1840 are missing.

[4]Miller, 253.

would have endured endless frauds and scams perpetrated by ticket agents, shippers, passage brokers, lodging-house keepers, porters, ship masters, and sailors.

Crossing the Pond

After many days or even weeks of delay, George and Elizabeth Chambers would have set sail from Liverpool for a voyage across the North Atlantic that typically took six weeks. Likely, they were cramped in steerage. Their vessel may have carried insufficient food and water. Their cooking facility may have been inadequate. Sanitation was probably poor. Boredom in all likelihood was constant except for the real possibility of storms and fires that may have made them fear for their lives. At best, they would have been very uncomfortable during the voyage.

Coastal Route

The first signs of land would have been a welcome sight and they would have thanked God for their deliverance upon their arrival in Eastport. Mindful that the weather would soon be changing and it was crucial they arrive at their final destination before winter, it is doubtful George and Elizabeth Chambers lingered very long in Eastport. Instead, they probably opted for passage on a schooner bound for Philadelphia. The coastal route typically took about 6 days.

ASSIMILATION IN AMERICA.

Having arrived safely in Philadelphia, George and Elizabeth Chambers probably secured temporary lodging near the Schuylkill River with family or friends already living in the area.

Based on information contained in the Philadelphia city directories, the Chambers family lived at the following locations in the early years:

1843   George Chambers shoemaker Schuylkill Front & High Street [later 22nd & Market]
1844   George Chambers shoemaker Schuylkill Front & High Street [later 22nd & Market]
1845   George Chambers shoemaker Schuylkill 2nd bel Filbert Street [later 21st bel Cuthbert]

George Chambers soon sought work as a shoemaker. It is unclear whether he brought his shoe making skills with him from Ireland or whether he acquired them in Philadelphia working as an apprentice. It is also unknown whether he worked in a shoeshop or at the Schuylkill Arsenal which was a major employer occupying eight acres of land near the Grays Ferry Road in South Philadelphia.

In those days, the Schuylkill Arsenal was a manufacturing center for every type of supply needed by soldiers in the Army of the United States including their coats, shirts, pantaloons, stockings, overcoats, shoes, gloves, mittens, caps, helmets, plumes, and ornaments. It was a very large workshop employing anywhere from 700 to 1200 women and about 150 men.[5]

George Chambers was still working as a shoemaker as late as July 23, 1850, when the family was enumerated in the 1850 census as follows:

PENNSYLVANIA, PHILADELPHIA, NORTH WARD:

George Chambers	35	M	Shoemaker	Ireland
Elizabeth	33	F		do
George	9	M		Penna
William	8	M		do
Emma	6	F		do
Charles	18	M	Laborer	Maine
John	16	M	Laborer	Penna[6]

George and Elizabeth Chambers lived near the Schuylkill River waterfront for most of their married life. Evidence suggests that sometime after 1850 George Chambers took advantage of his proximity to the Schuylkill waterfront to begin working as a boatman. His two sons appear to have joined him there as boatmen as soon as they were old enough to work. The listings in the city directories were as follows:

1851   William bel Vine Street [later 24th bel Vine], laborer[7] (inconclusive)
1855   Cuthbert below 23rd Street, boatman[8]
1860   Fairmount Ave [later 25th Street], boatman[9] (inconclusive)
1861   2312 Chestnut, laborer[10]

RAISING A FAMILY IN PHILADELPHIA.

Eager for independence, steady employment, enough to eat, and a home to call their own, the Chambers family may have quickly shed old habits and loyalties. Indeed, they may even have abandoned their traditional Anglican or Dissenter faith in favor of a comfortable self-

---

[5]Scharf and Westcott, *History of Philadelphia: 1609-1884*, 3 volumes (Philadelphia, Pennsylvania: Everts and Company, 1884), 1015, 2288.

[6]1850 U.S. Census (population), Pennsylvania, Philadelphia County, City of Philadelphia, North Ward, page 209, National Archives Microfilm Publication M432, Roll 817. NOTE: The relationship of George Chambers to Charles and John Chambers is unknown.

[7]1851 Philadelphia City Directory

[8]1855 Philadelphia City Directory.

[9]1860 Philadelphia City Directory.

[10]1861 Philadelphia City Directory.

sufficiency that included conversion to Methodism.[11] Despite their high hopes of achieving the American dream, the lives of the Chambers family members were beset by tragedy and early death.

Elizabeth Chambers - Mother

Elizabeth Chambers was a wife, mother and homemaker. She is only known to have had three children. Her oldest child, George Washington Chambers, was born on February 22, 1841.[12] Her middle child, William Chambers, was born about 1842 and her youngest child, Emma Chambers, was born about 1844.[13] No record of their baptisms has yet been found.

Sadly, Elizabeth Chambers was the first of the family to pass away. Her death certificate states she died of dysentery, an inflammatory disease of the large intestine believed to be infectious. Dysentery was a scourge that killed many people. The passage from summer into autumn was considered to be the season when dysentery epidemics were most prevalent. Generally, the epidemics were attributed to neglect of well established sanitary rules.[14]

An obituary for Elizabeth Chambers appeared in the *Philadelphia Public Ledger* on Wednesday, October 8, 1862. It read as follows:

> CHAMBERS - On Monday evening the 6th instant, Mrs. Elizabeth Chambers, wife of George Chambers, in the 50th (sic) year of her age. The relatives and friends of the family are respectfully invited to attend the funeral from the residence of her husband, Twenty-fourth Street, three doors below Sansom on Thursday morning at 9 o'clock. [Washington papers please copy.][15]

It is unclear why the Washington, D.C., newspapers were asked to run her obituary other than to notify family members who may have been traveling, posted or living there at the time.

---

[11]Miller, 265.

[12]George Chambers and Annie A. Chambers, widow, Civil War Pension Application, SO 1304127, SC 1102701, WO 849418, WC 612527, Records of the Veterans Administration, Record Group 15, National Archives, Washington, D.C.

[13]1850 U.S. Census (population), Pennsylvania, Philadelphia County, City of Philadelphia, North Ward, page 209, National Archives Microfilm Publication M432, Roll 817.

[14]*Sanitary Commission - Report of a Committee of the Associate Members of the Sanitary Commission on Dysentery*, (Philadelphia, Pennsylvania: Collins, Printer, 1862), 3.

[15]Obituary, *Philadelphia Public Ledger*, Wednesday, October 8, 1862, p. 2.

Elizabeth Chambers was buried at Union Methodist Episcopal Cemetery.[16] The cemetery was then located in Philadelphia between 10th and 11th Streets north of Washington Avenue beside Machpelah Cemetery.[17] She remained there until 1902 when the Board of Health approved the removal of all those buried in the cemetery, including Elizabeth Chambers, to Arlington Cemetery in Delaware County, Pennsylvania.[18] Almost immediately thereafter, the cemetery ground was sold to a developer.[19]

William Chambers - Younger Son

William Chambers was a boatman. There is no evidence that he served during the Civil War. He died young never having married. He was killed instantly on August 31, 1866, in a work-related accident on the waterfront above the Falls of the Schuylkill. A brief account of the accident appeared in the *Philadelphia Public Ledger*. It read as follows:

> INSTANTLY KILLED - William Chambers, 21 (sic) years of age, was killed on Monday (sic) by the falling of a derrick at Shunk's Rock, above the Falls of the Schuylkill. The Coroner was notified.[20]

---

[16]Philadelphia Cemetery Returns, Machpelah (sic) Cemetery Interments for the Week Ending October 11, 1862, Philadelphia City Archives, Philadelphia, Pennsylvania 19108 also contains the list of burials in Methodist Episcopal Union including Elizabeth Chambers who was living at Beach (aka 24th) Street below Sansom at the time of her death.

[17]Charles R. Barker, *A Register of the Burying Grounds of Philadelphia*, 5 volumes (Philadelphia, Pennsylvania: n.p., 1943), Volume 1, Map 8, # 53.

[18]News Story, *Philadelphia Inquirer*, Wednesday, January 8, 1902, p. 6.

> TO REMOVE OLD GRAVEYARD
> Bodies Will Be Taken From Union Cemetery
>
> Upon request of the Union M.E. Church, the Board of Health yesterday granted them permission to remove 2500 bodies from the old Union Cemetery at Tenth street and Washington avenue, to Arlington Cemetery, Delaware county. The cemetery was closed in 1890 by order of the Board of Health. The site will be used for building purposes.

[19]Charles R. Barker, *A Register of the Burying Grounds of Philadelphia*, 5 volumes (Philadelphia, Pennsylvania: n.p., 1943), Volume 1, p. 133, refers to Deed Book WSV 73 p. 190 with a sale date of July 1, 1902.

[20]News Story, *Philadelphia Public Ledger*, Wednesday, September 5, 1866, p. 2.

The coroner's certificate states that William Chambers was "crushed by a stone."[21] The news account of the Coroner's Inquest read as follows:

CORONER'S INQUEST - The Coroner held an inquest yesterday on the body of William Chambers, 21 (sic) years old, who was killed by the falling of a derrick at Shunk's Rock, above the Falls. A verdict in accordance with the facts was rendered.[22]

His obituary appeared in the *Philadelphia Public Ledger* on Saturday, September 1, 1866. It read as follows:

CHAMBERS – On the 31st ult. WILLIAM, son of George and the late Eliza Chambers, aged 21 (sic) years. The relatives and friends of the family are respectfully invited to attend the funeral, from the residence of his brother in law, John Clark, No. 1 Simes Street, between Market and Chesnut (sic) below twenty-third, on Sunday afternoon at 3 o'clock.[23]

The sudden and unexpected death of William Chambers must have shocked and devastated the Chambers family. At first, plans were made to inter him in Union Methodist Episcopal Cemetery where his mother was buried, but that arrangement appears to have been changed to Odd Fellows Cemetery where he was buried on September 2, 1866, in the Strangers' Ground.[24,25] Little else is known about the brief life of William Chambers except that on April 9, 1951, (85 years after he was buried in the Odd Fellows Cemetery) his remains were removed to Mount Peace Cemetery where they still rest today in an unmarked grave.[26]

---

[21]Philadelphia Cemetery Returns, Odd Fellows Cemetery Interments for the Week Ending August (sic) 7, 1866, Philadelphia City Archives, Philadelphia, Pennsylvania, Coroner's Certificate for Wm Chambers says Cause of Death: Crushed by a Stone.

[22]News Story, *Philadelphia Public Ledger*, Tuesday, September 4, 1866.

[23]Obituary, *Philadelphia Public Ledger*, Saturday, September 1, 1866.

[24]Philadelphia Cemetery Returns, Odd Fellows Cemetery Interments for the Week Ending August (sic) 7, 1866, Philadelphia City Archives, Philadelphia, Pennsylvania, Coroner's Certificate for Wm Chambers says Place of Burial: Union Methodist [crossed out] Odd Fellows [handwritten below].

[25]Pennsylvania and New Jersey, Church and Town Records, 1708-1985, Historical Society of Pennsylvania, Odd Fellows Cemetery, Index to Register of Interments, Register Book 21242, p. 869, Strangers Ground, burial on September 1, (sic) 1866.

[26]Pennsylvania and New Jersey, Church and Town Records, 1708-1985, Historical Society of Pennsylvania, Mount Peace Cemetery, Record of Removals, April 9, 1951. The Odd Fellows Cemetery Company owns Mount Peace Cemetery. In 1865, the company bought a 50

After the death of his wife, Elizabeth, George Chambers and his family appear to have moved to 2301 Simes Street. The move may have coincided with the marriage of his daughter, Emma, to John Clark.

George Chambers was probably living at 2301 Simes Street on March 24, 1865, when he is believed to have filed a Declaration of Intent to become a citizen of the United States. The declaration was filed before the Prothonotary of the District Court of the City and County of Philadelphia.[27] Unfortunately, there is no record that George Chambers ever completed the naturalization process in any court - city, county, state or federal - located in the City of Philadelphia.[28,29]

George Chambers died on May 3, 1868 from pleuro-pneumonia. His obituary appeared in the *Philadelphia Public Ledger*. It read as follows:

> CHAMBERS - On the 3[d] inst., GEORGE CHAMBERS, aged 65 (sic) years. The relatives and friends of the family are respectfully invited to attend the funeral, from his late residence, No. 2301 Simes street, below Market this day, 5th inst., at 12 o'clock.[30]

Having endured the death of his wife, Elizabeth, and of his younger son, William, George Chambers was laid to rest at Union Methodist Episcopal Cemetery.[31] In 1902, the cemetery

---

acre tract of land from an estate known as "Mount Peace" for use as a second cemetery. Mount Peace Cemetery is located at 31st and Lehigh Avenue in Philadelphia.

[27]Philadelphia County District Court Declarations of Intent, p 472, Philadelphia City Archives, 401 North Broad Street, Suite 942, Philadelphia, Pennsylvania 19108, lists a George Chambers, aged 52, a native of Ireland now residing in the City of Philadelphia, who submitted his Declaration of Intent on March 24, 1865.

[28]Index to Naturalization Petitions in the U.S. Circuit and District Courts for the Eastern District of Pennsylvania, 1795- 1951, National Archives Microfilm Publication M1248, Roll 2.

[29]William P. Filby, *Philadelphia Naturalization Records: An Index to Records of Aliens' Declarations of Intention and/or Oaths of Allegiance, 1789-1880*, (Detroit, Michigan: Gale Research Company, 1982), 90.

[30]Obituary, *Philadelphia Public Ledger*, Tuesday, May 5, 1868.

[31]Philadelphia Cemetery Returns, Methodist Episcopal Union Cemetery Interments for the Week Ending May 9, 1868, Philadelphia City Archives, Philadelphia, Pennsylvania 19108 say that George Chambers was living at 2301 Simes Street at the time of his death.

ground was sold to a developer so George Chambers and his wife, Elizabeth, were disinterred and removed, together with 2500 others, to Delaware County where they were re-interred at Arlington Cemetery.[32]

Emma Chambers - Only Daughter

Emma Chambers married John Clark, the son of Thomas and Ann Clark. John Clark's father was a boatman who died on July 19, 1850, in a weather-related work accident on the Schuylkill canal at Flat Rock above Manayunk.[33] The year the couple married is unknown but was probably about 1864.

Emma (Chambers) Clark appears to have converted to the Roman Catholic faith after her marriage to John Clark. Her name appeared in the Clark Family Bible, a Catholic version, along with birth entries for five members of the Clark family.[34,35]

The couple had at least three children - Thomas Clark, Thomas John Clark and Emma Rose Clark. The children were born in Philadelphia in October 1865 and on January 3, 1867,

------

[32]News Story, *Philadelphia Inquirer*, Wednesday, January 8, 1902, p. 6, "TO REMOVE OLD GRAVEYARD - Bodies Will Be Taken From Union Cemetery."

[33] News Story, *Philadelphia Public Ledger*, Saturday, July 20, 1850.

> FATAL RESULT FROM THE STORM
> Yesterday morning, between one and two o'clock, a canal boat, lying in the Schuylkill canal, at Flat Rock, above Manayunk, was capsized, and four men, who were in the cabin at the time, were drowned. Their names were Thomas Clark, Edward Clark, Peter Farley, and Wm Delaney, and all residents of the city and the neighborhood of Pine and Lombard streets and the Schuylkill river. Their bodies were hooked out of the boat yesterday morning and an inquest held upon them by the coroner. The first three named have left families. The boat was loaded with limestone from the vicinity of Norristown.

[34]William Edwards, Civil War Pension Application, SO 52835, SC 34984, Records of the Veterans Administration, Record Group 15, National Archives, Washington, D.C., states that in 1910 the Clark Family Bible was in the possession of William Scott Edwards the brother-in-law of John Clark. The only transcribed entry states Mrs. Emma Clark died on December 26, (sic) 1883.

[35]Kathryn Chambers Torpey, *The Edwards/Scott Family History*, (Alexandria, Virginia: Torpey Books, 2016), 30.

and February 28, 1871, respectively.[36,37,38]

John Clark was working as an apprentice glassblower as early as 1860.[39] Thereafter, John Clark was listed in the Philadelphia city directories as follows:

1866	2301 Simes Street, laborer (listed as Allen Clark)	
1867	2301 Simes Street, glassblower	
1868	2301 Simes Street, glassblower	
1875	2301 Simes Street, glassblower	
1876	2301 Simes Street, glassblower	
1879	2301 Simes Street, glassblower	
1880	2301 Simes Street, glassblower	
1883	3623 Filbert Street, glassblower, WP	
1884	3623 Filbert Street, glassblower, WP	

During their entire married life, John Clark appears to have worked as a glassblower while Emma raised the children.[40,41] Sadly, Emma (Chambers) Clark died while her two surviving children were still relatively young. The cause of her death was Congestion of the Brain.[42] Her obituary appeared in the *Philadelphia Public Ledger* on December 28, 1883. It read as follows:

---

[36]Pennsylvania and New Jersey, Church and Town Records, 1708-1985, Historical Society of Pennsylvania, Old Cathedral Cemetery, Register of Interments, says: Thomas Clarke (sic), 2 weeks old, burial November 9, 1865 in Section B, Range 4, Lot 26.

[37]Death Certificate for Thomas John Clark, January 25, 1949, # 7302 & # 1942, Pennsylvania Division of Vital Statistics, New Castle, Pennsylvania 16103, says that Thomas John Clark was born January 3, 1865 (sic).

[38]1871 Birth Register, City of Philadelphia, page 30, Philadelphia City Archives, Philadelphia, Pennsylvania.

[39]1860 U.S. Census (population), Pennsylvania, Philadelphia County, City of Philadelphia, Ward 7, page 669, National Archives Microfilm Publication M653, Roll 1157.

[40]1870 U.S. Census (population), Pennsylvania, Philadelphia County, City of Philadelphia, Ward 9, page 98, National Archives Microfilm Publication M593, Roll 1394.

[41]1880 U.S. Census (population), Pennsylvania, Philadelphia County, City of Philadelphia, Ward 9, E.D. 164, page 120D, sheet 16, line 3, National Archives Microfilm Publication T9, Roll 1171.

[42]Philadelphia Cemetery Returns, Old Cathedral Cemetery Interments for the Week Ending December 28, 1883, Philadelphia City Archives, Philadelphia, Pennsylvania 19108 says Emma Clark died on December 26, (sic) 1883.

CLARK - On the 25th (sic) inst., Emma, wife of John Clark, aged 34 (sic) years. The relatives and friends of the family are respectfully invited to attend the funeral on Saturday morning at 8 o'clock from her husband's residence 3623 Filbert Street, W.P. High Mass at St. James Church. To proceed to Old Cathedral.[43]

Emma (Chambers) Clark was interred at Old Cathedral Cemetery in a plot belonging to her husband, John Clark.[44],[45] After the death of Emma (Chambers) Clark, her widower husband appears to have lived in South Philadelphia at the home of his brother-in-law, William Scott Edwards, for many years. John Clark's children probably lived there, too, as did his mother, Ann Clark. During that time, John Clark was listed in the Philadelphia city directories as follows:

1885	John Clark, glassblower, h 2502 Pine
1887	John S. Clark, glassblower, h 2502 Pine
1888	John Clark, glassblower, h 2502 Pine
1890	John Clark, laborer, h 2502 Pine
1891	John H. Clark, blower, h 2502 Pine
1892	John H. Clark, blower, h 2502 Pine
1893	John H. Clark, blower, h 2502 Pine
1894	John Clark, blower, h 2502 Pine
1895	John Clark, laborer, h 2502 Pine
1898	Jno. Clark, blower, h 2402 (sic) Pine

John Clark's mother, Ann Clark, died on October 1, 1904, at the home of her son-in-law, William Scott Edwards, 2502 Pine Street.[46],[47] She was laid to rest in the Clark family plot in Old

---

[43]Obituary, *Philadelphia Public Ledger*, Friday, December 28, 1883, page 2, and Saturday, December 29, 1883, page 2.

[44]Letter dated December 23, 1997, from Veronica T. Johnson, Assistant Director, Catholic Cemeteries Office, 111 South 38th Street, Philadelphia, Pennsylvania 19104-3179 concerning the plot owned by John Clark, husband of Emma Chambers Clark, (Section B, Range 4, Lot 26) at Old Cathedral Cemetery.

[45]Pennsylvania and New Jersey, Church and Town Records, 1708-1985, Historical Society of Pennsylvania, Old Cathedral Cemetery, Register of Interments, says the body of Emma Clark was placed in the vault and burial was on January 29, 1884 in Section B, Range 4, Lot 26.

[46]Return of a Death in the City of Philadelphia, Ann Clark, October 1, 1904, 2502 Pine Street, Ward 7, Philadelphia City Archives, Philadelphia, Pennsylvania 19108.

[47]Obituary, *Philadelphia Public Ledger*, Monday, October 3, 1904, p. 9, says:

CLARK - On October 1, 1904, ANN, wife of the late Thomas C. Clark, aged 90. Relatives and friends of the family are invited to attend the funeral Tuesday at

Cathedral Cemetery belonging to her son. No definitive information has been found about the death of John Clark except that he does not appear to have been buried in the family plot he owned at Old Cathedral Cemetery.[48]

George Washington Chambers - Older Son

Being the oldest child of George and Elizabeth Chambers, George Washington Chambers was the first of the Chambers family born in America. Despite being uneducated and illiterate, he always did the right thing as a son, husband, and father. He was an honorable man who worked hard, served his county in time of war, and always put the needs of his family before his own.

PHILADELPHIA DURING THE WAR YEARS

In 1861 and the following three years, Philadelphia was absorbed in one thought and one effort only - the War of the Rebellion.

The streets were filled with marching men who came to join the local regiments. The sound of the fife and drum was heard everywhere. Regiments passed through the city almost daily on their way south. The public squares and the armories were full of soldiers who were receiving their first instruction from the drill masters. The navy yard was crowded with workmen. At the Schuylkill Arsenal, on Grays Ferry Road, and elsewhere, thousands of women were employed sewing uniforms. Flannel garments, socks, handkerchiefs, as well as many things that were valuable, and many that were completely useless were prepared for the departing troops. Wagon makers, cloth manufacturers, gun and powder manufacturers, and many other city industries turned their attention to producing military supplies.[49]

It was in this highly charged atmosphere that George Washington Chambers came to enlist in the 24th Regiment of the Pennsylvania Volunteer Infantry. He enlisted in Philadelphia on May 1, 1861, for a period of three months. He claimed to be 21 years old at the time and

---

8:30 AM from the residence of her son-in-law Mr. William Edwards, 2502 Pine street. High mass of Requiem at St. Patrick's Church. Interment at Cathedral Cemetery.

[48]Letter dated December 23, 1997, from Veronica T. Johnson, Assistant Director, Catholic Cemeteries Office, 111 South 38th Street, Philadelphia, Pennsylvania 19104-3179 concerning the plot owned by John Clark, (Section B, Range 4, Lot 26) at Old Cathedral Cemetery.

[49]Ellis Paxson Oberholtzer, *Philadelphia: A History of the City and its People; A Record of 225 Years*, 4 volumes (Philadelphia, Pennsylvania: S.J. Clarke, 1912), 361.

living at 23rd and Cuthbert Streets.[50,51]

The 24th Regiment of the Pennsylvania Volunteer Infantry was principally recruited in Philadelphia, the nucleus of its organization being the Second Regiment, Second Brigade, First Division of the Pennsylvania militia, which already existed under the act of 1858. Recruiting commenced on April 23, 1861, and was pursued with vigor by the company officers. Recruitment was completed and the men were mustered into the service of the United States on May, 7, 1861, by Captain Thomas Neill, of the regular army. The recruits were principally of Irish birth or descent.[52]

Undoubtedly, George Washington Chambers was part of a company of green recruits few of whom had any idea of what lay ahead of them. Most were responding to President Lincoln's proclamation of April 15, 1861, in which he called forth the state militias to suppress "combinations" in seven states "too powerful to be suppressed by the ordinary course of judicial proceedings." The patriotic response was enormous and, amid the storm of indignation which shook both sides, the citizens of Philadelphia vigorously prepared for war.[53] All Pennsylvania troops were put under the command of Major General Robert Patterson, while the Philadelphia brigades were placed under the immediate direction of General George Cadwalader.[54]

After the recruits were mustered-in, the first camp of rendezvous for the 24th Regiment was at Hestonville, near the outskirts of the city of Philadelphia, where the men were engaged in various duties of the camp and in squad and company drills. Subsequently, the regiment moved to Suffolk Park where military instruction was continued. Fortunately for the men, the citizens of Philadelphia continued to provide them with liberal supplies of woollen stockings, underclothing and other items which helped sustain them in their exposure to inclement weather during the

---

[50]Union Compiled Military Service Record for George Chambers, Co. D, 24th Pennsylvania Volunteer Infantry, Records of the Adjutant General's Office, Record Group 94, National Archives, Washington, D.C.

[51]George Chambers and Annie A. Chambers, widow, Civil War Pension Application SO 1304127, SC 1102701, WO 849418, WC 612527, Records of the Veterans Administration, Record Group 15, National Archives, Washington, D.C.

[52]Samuel P. Bates, *History of the Pennsylvania Volunteers 1861-1865*, 5 volumes (Harrisburg, Pennsylvania: B. Singerly, State Printer, 1869), 218.

[53]J.G. Randall and David Herbert Donald, *The Civil War and Reconstruction*, (Lexington, Massachusetts: D.C. Heath and Company, 1969), 177.

[54]Oberholtzer, 361.

coming campaign in the Shenandoah Valley.[55]

Early in June, the regiment broke camp at Suffolk Park and moved to Chambersburg, Pennsylvania, where it was stationed a short distance from the town. On June 21, the regiment marched to Hagerstown, Maryland, and from there, on the following day, to Camp Porter, where it was assigned to the Fifth Brigade of the Second Division under the command of General Patterson. Its primary mission in the campaign in the Shenandoah Valley was to prevent the Confederate forces stationed in Winchester, Virginia, then under the command of General Joseph E. Johnston, from reinforcing General P.G.T. Beauregard, commander of the main Confederate army at Manassas Junction.[56]

In pursuit of this mission, the Union forces under General Patterson advanced and almost immediately encountered the Confederates under the command of General Johnston. The 24th Regiment, which formed part of the right wing of the advancing column, moved by road to Hedgeville where it encountered the Confederate cavalry. Later, rejoining the main column at Hainseville, the 24th Regiment moved to Martinsburg and subsequently to Bunker Hill.

While stationed at Bunker Hill, reconnaissance was made by the 24th Regiment of all the ways leading to Winchester where General Johnston and the Confederates were still located, but every way was found to be blocked by felled timber and other obstructions. No progress having been made in achieving their objective, the Union forces marched to Charlestown. Thus, General Johnston was successful in evading General Patterson's Union forces and moving his troops, via the Manassas Gap Railroad, in the direction of Manassas Junction. They arrived on July 20 and 21 and marched directly from the trains into the Battle of Bull Run (also known as First Manassas).[57]

The 24th Regiment, after remaining a few days at Charlestown, moved on to Harper's Ferry. The original term of their service had now nearly expired and preparations were made to return home. But General Patterson, finding that the rapid disbandment of the three month regiments was likely to leave him without an adequate force to hold his position in the Shenandoah Valley, made an appeal to the regiment to remain in service until replacements arrived. This request was agreed to and the men remained in place for two weeks beyond the original period of their enlistment. At the expiration of this time, the 24th Regiment was ordered to move by rail, via Baltimore, to Philadelphia, where it arrived on August 9, 1861, and was soon after mustered out of service.[58]

---

[55]Bates, 218.

[56]Randall and Donald, 199.

[57]Bates, 219.

[58]Bates, 219.

Undoubtedly, George Washington Chambers was glad to arrive home alive. His military service record indicates that he was due pay from the time of his enrollment. There is no indication, however, whether he was ever paid. Despite the parade, the welcome home ceremonies, and heavy recruitment efforts, there is no indication that George Washington Chambers had any interest in re-enlistment.

Everywhere he went after his return home, the conversation was about the war - of battles expected, of conflicts past, of those who had died, and of those who escaped. Other news seemed of little consequence. The campaign in the Shenandoah Valley in which George Washington Chambers had participated in the summer of 1861 was of major interest and the defeat at the Battle of Bull Run was a stunning blow.[59] It seemed as though there was no end in sight. Everywhere, young men could be seen shooting at targets. On the outskirts of the city, large numbers of men were assembled in tents in camps awaiting orders which would send them south to the front lines. Weeping women accompanied recruits to the railroad station while preachers blessed the regimental colors. Some of the women, acting individually or in small groups, soon began providing soldiers in transit with coffee and sandwiches at the depot established at the foot of Washington street. This charity, on the part of a few women, soon led to the establishment of the two great Refreshment Saloons - the Union Volunteer and the Cooper Shop - which hundreds of thousands of Union soldiers always remembered gratefully.[60]

Even though the city of Philadelphia was far removed from the scene of battle, the suffering of its citizens cannot be minimized. Hope for a speedy end to the war was endlessly deferred while sacrifices were increasingly demanded. Almost everyone in the city had a relative or a close friend who was away at war and whose fate remained unknown or who was subject to the drafts that took place in the city between 1863 and 1865. Even the invasion of Pennsylvania in the summer of 1863 coupled with the expressed determination of General Robert E. Lee to carry the war into the North, produced in Philadelphia such emotional distress as to make every previous experience of the city's life seem trivial by comparison.[61]

Having satisfied his military service commitment early in the war, George Washington Chambers stayed put and resumed work as a laborer somewhere in the vicinity of his home located at 2312 Chestnut Street.[62] Judging from its location - just a block and a half from the Schuylkill River - he probably returned to work as the boatman loading and unloading vessels

---

[59]John Russell Young, editor, *Memorial History of the City of Philadelphia: From its First Settlement to the Year 1895*, 2 volumes (New York, New York: New York History, 1895, 1898), 522.

[60]Oberholtzer, 315.

[61]Young, 528.

[62]1861 Philadelphia City Directory.

docked along the river.

Mercifully, the war finally came to an end in April of 1865 with the collapse of the Confederacy and the surrender at Appomattox. The troops eventually came home and everyone tried their best to resume living a normal life.

WORKING ALONG THE SCHUYLKILL RIVER WATERFRONT

As best can be determined, George Washington Chambers probably worked as a boatman for most of his life.[63] As a boatman, (also known as a longshoreman) he would have worked manual labor in a gang that loaded and unloaded cargo from ships and barges docked along the Schuylkill River.

Whenever a ship arrived in port, it was usually assigned to a General Agent by the owner. The General Agent was licensed to handle all business with respect to the ship including hiring a stevedore to load or unload it. The stevedoring companies that George Washington Chambers worked for probably handled just about any type of cargo including logs, lumber, bagged goods, coal, pig iron, stone blocks, grain, lime, salt, fertilizer, and so forth on any type of vessel that docked along the Schuylkill River. The stevedore typically owned all the equipment necessary to load and unload the ships including rope, wire slings, and nets for handling the cargo, all sorts of wooden pallets and big pie plates, dollies and hand trucks, and any other imaginable piece of equipment for cargo handling.

The stevedore was also responsible for hiring the boatmen. Boatmen were known as casual labor in those days thus they were only paid for the hours they worked. They were always paid in cash and the stevedoring companies probably kept few, if any, records concerning the men who worked for them on any given day.

When a ship was slated to "work cargo," the boatmen "shaped-up" at the head of the pier. During the "shape," the stevedore's hiring boss simply pointed his finger at a man who then walked onto the pier and gathered together with the other boatmen picked for the "hatch gang." If a boatman did not "get the nod," he went home or, if another ship was due to arrive or the stevedore was going to work another "hatch" in the afternoon, the boatmen waited for the next "shape."[64]

Unquestionably, longshoring was a brutal occupation. In those days, the job largely

---

[63]George Chambers and Annie A. Chambers, widow, Civil War Pension Application SO 1304127, SC 1102701, WO 849418, WC 612527, Records of the Veterans Administration, Record Group 15, National Archives, Washington, D.C.

[64]E-mail dated April 7, 2000, from the late William Scott Chambers, 325 N.W. 95th Avenue, Plantation, Florida 33324.

involved manual labor. The boatmen would have worked aboard the ship in the hold or alongside the ship in the yard loading and unloading heavy cargo from the slings or the pallets, whatever its form - loose, boxed, bagged or barrels. Thus, in order to survive for very long as a boatman, George Washington Chambers would have needed to be a tough, muscular man capable of consistently performing a strenuous job despite being only five feet, five-and-a-half inches tall and weighing only about 130 pounds.

George Washington Chambers indicated in a deposition in support of his application for a Civil War pension, that he worked for many different people (i.e., stevedores) over the course of his lifetime, at no particular place for any length of time, but wherever he could get work. His deposition also attests to the ever present dangers of an occupation that left him handicapped, but still ready and willing to work.

His first serious accident as a boatman probably occurred in July, 1885. The circumstances surrounding the accident were described by George Washington Chambers in his deposition of December 17, 1904:

> About 18 years ago, [I] cannot tell the year, it was in the Summer, I was loading stone blocks for paving streets in a big iron tub. [I] was down in the hold of a schooner and the iron handle of the tub came off and struck my big toe of [my] left foot. I went home, 2305 Symes (sic) Street between 23rd and 24th and between Chestnut and Market. My toe was amputated by Doctor Frederick Carrier who then lived on [the] West side of N. 16th between Filbert and Cuthbert. [I have] no idea where he is [now]. There were two doctors with him, names not known.

His wife, Annie Adam (Edwards) Chambers, also recalled the accident:

> He lost his great toe in [the] Summer of 1887, the Summer before the big blizzard (1888). [The] toe was amputated by Dr. Frederick Carrier at our home 2305 Symes (sic) Street.

Even the doctor who amputated George Washington Chambers' toe provided his account of the medical care he dispensed as a result of the accident:

> My record, now before me, shows that I saw a Mr. Chambers at 2305 Symes (sic) Street [on] July 20 1885. I have records of visits nearly every day for a month, and on August 8, 1885, I have entered "operation". I recall that it (sic) I amputated a toe, cannot recall just which toe, or on which foot. I have before us a bottle in which I preserved the toe, but the toe has been lost, the bottle bears a label which reads "George Chambers, Opr. 8-8-85."

The second bad accident appears to have occurred in June, 1892. It, too, was described by George Washington Chambers in his deposition of December 17, 1904:

> [I] cannot tell the year, it was about 10 years ago, [I] cannot tell the month or day of the month, it was in the Summer time. I was shoveling coal for W.C. Kirk &

16

Co. filling buckets in a canal boat to be hoisted up, on the Schuylkill River just below Chestnut Street bridge. A piece of coal flew from the shovel and struck me in the left eye. Luke Brannon, now on Ludlow Street between 30th and 31st, was working with me. No one else. I did not quit work for about 4 days and then I went to the University Hospital and was there 2 or 3 weeks under treatment for my eye. My sight of left eye was lost at once, [I] have never been able to see with that eye since. I did not say anything to Kirk & Co. about it.

His wife, Annie Adam (Edwards) Chambers, also provided her account of the second accident:

We have lived in this house (3223 Lombard Street) 10 years, moved here in the Spring or Summer 10 years ago. He lost the sight of his left eye the summer before that, [I] cannot tell [the] month, we then lived at 3211 St. James Street and his eye was treated at the University Hospital. He was a free patient. He has not been able to see at all with that eye since. Was shoveling coal when he lost his eye.

Their account was confirmed by the Special Examiner from the Bureau of Pensions who reviewed the hospital records and found that:

Referring to [the] date of [the] injury to [the] claimant's left eye, I found on the record of University Hospital the following entry, viz: "George Chambers, age 43, laborer, Philadelphia, admitted 6.28.92. Diagnosis, Hypopyon Keratitis.[65,66] Revised diagnosis, Operation Saniesch.[67] Result, improved. Discharged 7.16. 92." The attending surgeon was Dr. William F. Norris who has since died, and the resident physician informed me that they had no chart of the case and no further data than above quoted.

Obviously, a boatman was no stranger to accidents or other safety concerns. It is doubtful that stevedoring companies did much in those days to ensure accident-free docks and ships. It is also doubtful that George Washington Chambers belonged to a union or had any kind of accident insurance or medical insurance to supplement his lost wages or cover the cost of treatment when the accidents occurred. By his own account, he never even told his employer about the second accident and foolishly stayed on the job for four days before seeking medical treatment.

As the years wore on, George Washington Chambers' hard work earned him precious little in terms of pay increases or job advancement. In fact, according to his doctor, George Washington Chambers ended his working years in December, 1904, as a "stooped shouldered,

---

[65]Hypopyon, a kind of ulcer; an accumulation of pus in the cavity between the cornea and the lens of the eye.

[66]Keratitis, an inflammation of the cornea.

[67]Sanies, a thin, often greenish, discharge of pus and serum from a wound or ulcer.

narrow chested" man with a "huskiness of voice as if there was laryngitis" and suffering from consumption. According to his doctor, George Washington Chambers was hardly able to do any work, "but handling a gray rope" two or three days a week and, in the doctor's opinion, would never again be able to do manual labor because of the lung trouble.

After more than forty-five years on the Schuylkill River waterfront, George Washington Chambers retired in December, 1904, on a Civil War invalid pension that paid him $10.00 a quarter. He died from pulmonary tuberculosis (i.e., consumption) seventeen months later.[68]

MARRIED LIFE IN PHILADELPHIA.

Tying the Knot

George Washington Chambers married Annie Adam Edwards on July 4, 1866, at the Church of the Redemption, a Protestant Episcopal Church located at 22nd and Callowhill.[69,70] The ceremony was performed by the Reverend George A. Durborrow.[71] George Washington Chambers was 25 years old and Annie Adam Edwards was 19 years old at the time they married.

The Family Circle

Immediately after George Washington Chambers and Annie Adam Edwards were married, she appears to have joined her husband at 2301 Simes Street where they boarded with John and Emma (Chambers) Clark and their family for about three years.[72] John Clark was a glassblower who married George Washington Chambers' sister, Emma Chambers. Interestingly,

---

[68]Death Certificate for George Washington Chambers, May 9, 1906, # 12476 & # 49558, Pennsylvania Division of Vital Statistics, New Castle, Pennsylvania 16103.

[69]Church of the Redemption (Protestant Episcopal) Marriage Register, Historical Society of Pennsylvania, Philadelphia, Pennsylvania.

[70]1866 Marriage Register, City of Philadelphia, page 77, Philadelphia City Archives, Philadelphia, Pennsylvania.

[71]The Reverend George A. Durborrow officiated at many marriage ceremonies while he was the minister of the Church of the Redemption including those of Annie Adam (Edwards) Chambers' brothers, George Edwards and Robert Edwards. The Reverend Durborrow died on April 27, 1869, at the age of 47. According to his obituary, which appeared on page 2 of the *Philadelphia Public Ledger* on Saturday, May 1, 1869, he was buried at Laurel Hill Cemetery.

[72]George Chambers and Annie A. Chambers, widow, Civil War Pension Application SO 1304127, SC 1102701, WO 849418, WC 612527, Records of the Veterans Administration, Record Group 15, National Archives, Washington, D.C.

John Clark's sister, Rose Clark, later married Annie Adam Edwards' brother, William Scott Edwards. Thus, these three sets of siblings made for a very tight family circle whose cross connections appear to have survived into the early years of the 20th Century.[73]

Home Sweet Home

George Washington Chambers worked as a boatman for most of his married life so the Chambers family spent many years living in working-class neighborhoods on the east side of the Schuylkill River. This living arrangement put George Washington Chambers within easy walking distance of the wharfs where he worked.

The only clearly discernible breaks in this pattern occurred first in 1870 when George Washington Chambers took a job as a driver and second in 1871 when he moved his family away from the wharfs along the Schuylkill River waterfront to a neighborhood in North Philadelphia known as Brewerytown.

This move away from the river may have been made in connection with George Washington Chambers taking a job with one of the many beer breweries then located in North Philadelphia. In any event, this change in occupation appears to have been relatively short-lived as George Washington Chambers is known to have resumed work as a laborer (presumably as a boatman) as early as 1879.

In all the years of their marriage, George Washington Chambers and his wife, Annie Adam (Edwards) Chambers, never owned a home of their own. Instead, the family boarded or rented at the following locations throughout the years:

LOCATION	TIME PERIOD
2301 Simes [later Ludlow] Street[74,75]	1866 - 1869

---

[73]Kathryn Chambers Torpey, *The Edwards/Scott Family History*, (Alexandria, Virginia: Torpey Books, 2016), 22-36.

[74]The 1869 Philadelphia City Directory.

[75]George Chambers and Annie A. Chambers, widow, Civil War Pension Application SO 1304127, SC 1102701, WO 849418, WC 612527, Records of the Veterans Administration, Record Group 15, National Archives, Washington, D.C.

2302 Race Street[76,77,78]	1869 - 1871
2627 Mt. Pleasant Street[79]	1871
2305 Simes [later Ludlow] Street[80,81,82]	1879 - 1889
3211 St. James Street, WP[83]	1889 - 1894
3223 Marston [later Lombard] Street, WP[84,85,86]	1894 - 1906

Death of George Washington Chambers

George Washington Chambers died from tuberculosis on May 9, 1906, in Philadelphia. He was 65 years old. His obituary appeared in the *Philadelphia Public Ledger* as follows:

> CHAMBERS - On May 9, 1906, George W., husband of Annie Chambers, aged 65 years. The relatives and friends of the family are invited to attend the funeral services on Saturday afternoon at 2 o'clock at his late resident 3223 Lombard

---

[76]George Chambers and Annie A. Chambers, widow, Civil War Pension Application SO 1304127, SC 1102701, WO 849418, WC 612527, Records of the Veterans Administration, Record Group 15, National Archives, Washington, D.C.

[77]1870 U.S. Census (population), Second Enumeration, Pennsylvania, Philadelphia County, City of Philadelphia, Ward 10, page 34B, National Archives Microfilm Publication M593, Roll 1423.

[78]1870, 1871 Philadelphia City Directory.

[79]Obituary, *Philadelphia Public Ledger*, Monday November 20, 1871, p. 2 and Tuesday, November 21, 1871, p. 2, concerning the death of Eliza Jane Chambers, the infant daughter of George Washington and Annie Adam (Edwards) Chambers.

[80]Simes Street was renamed Ludlow Street in 1897.

[81]1879-1885 Philadelphia City Directory.

[82]1880 U.S. Census (population), Pennsylvania, Philadelphia County, City of Philadelphia, Ward 9, E.D. 164, page 120D, sheet 16, line 22, National Archives Microfilm Publication T9, Roll 1171.

[83]1889 - 1893, 1894 (W^m) Philadelphia City Directory.

[84]1895, 1896 (W^m), 1897-1898, 1900-1903, 1904 (Geo E.), 1905-1906 City Directory.

[85]1897 Philadelphia City Directory says George Chambers 3233 (sic) Marston; William Chambers 3223 Marston. Marston Street was renamed Lombard Street in 1897.

[86]Death Certificate for George Washington Chambers, May 9, 1906, # 12476 & # 49558, Pennsylvania Division of Vital Statistics, New Castle, Pennsylvania 16103.

Street, West Philadelphia. Interment at Mt. Moriah Cemetery.[87]

George Washington Chambers was laid out in a black cloth casket with a cream satin lining and silver handles. He was wearing a brand new suit. The plate inscription on his casket read: George W. Chambers, February 22 1841 - May 9 1906. The Reverend William Oxtoby from Tabernacle Presbyterian Church at 37th and Chestnut Streets officiated at his funeral.[88]

After the ceremony, the funeral procession, consisting of a horse-drawn hearse followed by ten carriages, made its way to Mount Moriah Cemetery. There, George Washington Chambers was laid to rest in the Chambers family plot.[89] He was buried in an oiled chestnut case.[90]

According to family legend, a Civil War headstone was installed on his grave at the expense of the government, but there is none in evidence today.[91] Fortunately for his widow, Annie Adam (Edwards) Chambers, George Washington Chambers had a life insurance policy at the time he died.[92] The entire amount ($350.00) was needed to pay his doctors, funeral, burial, and other expenses associated with his illness and death. Since the life insurance policy was the only form of financial planning George Washington Chambers could afford, his widow was left destitute after he died so she applied for, and received, a Civil War widow's pension.[93]

[87]Obituary, *Philadelphia Public Ledger*, Thursday, May 10, 1906, p. 9; Friday, May 11, 1906, p. 9; and Saturday, May 12, 1906, p. 9.

[88]Oliver Bair Funeral Home Record for George W. Chambers, May 10, 1906, Genealogical Society of Pennsylvania, Philadelphia, Pennsylvania.

[89]Letter dated July 20, 1995, from Lydia M. Jones, Director, Mt. Moriah Cemetery, concerning the plot owned by George W. Chambers (Section 204, Lot 503).

[90]Oliver Bair Funeral Home Record for George W. Chambers, May 10, 1906, Genealogical Society of Pennsylvania, Philadelphia, Pennsylvania.

[91]Conversation (date unknown) with the late Mary Ann (McCauley) Chambers, widow of George Washington Chambers' grandson, Henry Grafe Chambers.

[92]Oliver Bair Funeral Home Record for George W. Chambers, May 10, 1906, Genealogical Society of Pennsylvania, Philadelphia, Pennsylvania.

[93]George Chambers and Annie A. Chambers, widow, Civil War Pension Application SO 1304127, SC 1102701, WO 849418, WC 612527, Records of the Veterans Administration, Record Group 15, National Archives, Washington, D.C.

DAUGHTERS OF GEORGE WASHINGTON CHAMBERS

Over the years, George Washington Chambers and his wife, Annie Adam (Edwards) Chambers, had five daughters - Eliza Jane, Lydia E., Emma C., Annie I., and Elizabeth H.

Eliza Jane Chambers

George Washington Chambers and Annie Adam (Edwards) Chambers' oldest daughter, Eliza Jane Chambers, may have been named after George Washington Chambers' mother, Elizabeth Chambers. The baby was born in Philadelphia on October 23, 1869 and she was baptized at the Church of the Redemption located at 22nd and Callowhill on January 9, 1870.[94,95]

At about the time Eliza Jane was born, George Washington Chambers must have decided that sharing a house with his sister, Emma (Chambers) Clark, and her family was getting too crowded so he moved his family from 2301 Simes Street to 2302 Race Street where he and his wife, Annie Adam (Edwards) Chambers, finally had a home of their own.[96,97] It is believed that shortly thereafter George Washington Chambers unexpectedly moved his family to a neighborhood in North Philadelphia known as Brewerytown. It was there that Eliza Jane Chambers died, suddenly, on November 18, 1871. She was only two years old. Her obituary appeared in the *Philadelphia Public Ledger* as follows:

> CHAMBERS - On the 18th inst., of inflammation of the lungs, Eliza Jane, daughter of George W. and Annie A. Chambers, age 2 years, 25 days. The relatives and friends of the family are respectfully invited to attend the funeral from the residence of her parents 2627 Mt. Pleasant (west of Girard College) on Tuesday afternoon at 1 o'clock. Interment at Mt. Moriah Cemetery.[98]

---

[94]George Chambers and Annie A. Chambers, widow, Civil War Pension Application SO 1304127, SC 1102701, WO 849418, WC 612527, Records of the Veterans Administration, Record Group 15, National Archives, Washington, D.C.

[95]Church of the Redemption (Protestant Episcopal) Baptismal Register, Historical Society of Pennsylvania, Philadelphia, Pennsylvania.

[96]1870 U.S. Census (population), First Enumeration, Pennsylvania, Philadelphia County, City of Philadelphia, Ward 10, page 417, National Archives Microfilm Publication M593, Roll 1395.

[97]1870 U.S. Census (population), Second Enumeration, Pennsylvania, Philadelphia County, City of Philadelphia, Ward 10, page 34B, National Archives Microfilm Publication M593, Roll 1423.

[98]Obituary. *Philadelphia Public Ledger*, Monday, November 20, 1871, p. 2 and Tuesday, November 21, 1871, p. 2.

After his daughter died, George Washington Chambers bought a plot at Mount Moriah Cemetery where Eliza Jane Chambers was laid to rest.[99]

Lydia E. Chambers

Lydia E. Chambers was born on February 27, 1872, in Philadelphia.[100,101] From the time she was a little girl, she was known to everyone as Lydie or Aunt Lydie to her nieces and nephews.[102]

MARRIAGE TO LEONARD H. SCHMIDT/SMITH. Her first marriage was to Leonard H. Schmidt who was also known as Leonard H. Smith. They were married on August 25, 1909, at Hope Presbyterian Church located at 33rd and Wharton Streets.[103] How Lydia E. Chambers may have met her husband is unknown, but, in 1904, he witnessed at least two depositions contained in George Washington Chambers' Civil War pension file. At the time of their marriage, Leonard H. Schmidt/Smith was living at 1308 South 33rd Street and Lydia E. Chambers was living with her sister, Emma (Chambers) Spence, at 2823 Wharton Street. After their marriage, the couple moved to 3022 Titan Street.[104] All three of these addresses are in close proximity in the Grays Ferry section of South Philadelphia.

Leonard H. Schmidt/Smith was born in Germany on July 13, 1878, and immigrated to the

---

[99]Letter dated July 20, 1995, from Lydia M. Jones, Director, Mt. Moriah Cemetery concerning the plot owned by George W. Chambers (Section 204, Lot 503).

[100]George Chambers and Annie A. Chambers, widow, Civil War Pension Application SO 1304127, SC 1102701, WO 849418, WC 612527, Records of the Veterans Administration, Record Group 15, National Archives, Washington, D.C.

[101]Affidavit of Applicant for Marriage License # 240839, July 13, 1909, (Leonard H. Smith & Lydia E. Chambers), City of Philadelphia, Philadelphia City Archives, Philadelphia, Pennsylvania says Lydia E. Chambers was born February 28, 1878.

[102]Conversation on November 29, 1996, with the late Josephine Thompson Marshall, 121 Reillywood Avenue, Haddonfield, New Jersey 08033.

[103]Affidavit of Applicant for Marriage License # 240839, July 13, 1909, (Leonard H. Smith & Lydia E. Chambers), City of Philadelphia, Philadelphia City Archives, Philadelphia, Pennsylvania.

[104]1910 U.S. Census (population), Pennsylvania, Philadelphia County, City of Philadelphia, Ward 36, E.D. 902, page 2B, line 81, Family Number 37, National Archives Microfilm Publication T624, Roll 1407, Leonard F. Smith, 3022 Titan Street.

United States in 1883 or 1884 when he was approximately seven years old.[105] He worked as a machinist at an iron manufactory.[106,107]

Leonard H. Schmidt/Smith died on February 14, 1915, from tuberculosis.[108] His obituary read as follows:

> SCHMIDT. Feb. 14, 1915. LEONARD H., husband of Lydia E. Schmidt (nee Chambers), aged 37 years. Funeral services on Thursday, at 2 P.M., at his late residence, 3115 Wharton st. Interment private at Mount Moriah Cemetery. Friends are invited Wednesday, from 7 to 9 P.M.[109]

He was buried in Mount Moriah Cemetery in the Schmidt family plot.[110] Buried with him were his parents, Ernest and Caroline Schmidt, and at least four of his siblings.[111,112,113]

---

[105]1900 U.S. Census (population), Pennsylvania, Philadelphia County, City of Philadelphia, Ward 36, E.D. 933, page 1A, line 37, National Archives Microfilm Publication T623, Roll 1477, Ernest and Caroline Smith, 1319 Hollywood Street, says 1883. Also, 1910 U.S. Census (population), Pennsylvania, Philadelphia County, City of Philadelphia, Ward 36, E.D. 902, page 2B, line 81, Family Number 37, National Archives Microfilm Publication T624, Roll 1407, Leonard F. Smith, 3022 Titan Street, says 1884.

[106]1910 U.S. Census (population), Pennsylvania, Philadelphia County, City of Philadelphia, Ward 36, E.D. 902, page 2B, line 81, Family Number 37, National Archives Microfilm Publication T624, Roll 1407, Leonard F. Smith, 3022 Titan Street.

[107]News Story, *Philadelphia Inquirer*, Wednesday, February 11, 1914, p. 6, and p. 16, "Record of the Courts - Common Pleas." NOTE: There is some inconclusive speculation that at some point in his life Leonard H. Smith may have worked in the rubber industry because in 1914 a man with the same name obtained a verdict of $7,000 against the Philadelphia Rubber Works Company for permanent personal injuries sustained while in the defendant's employ.

[108]Death Certificate for Leonard Schmidt, February 14, 1915, # 3885, Pennsylvania Division of Vital Statistics, New Castle, Pennsylvania.

[109]Obituary, *Philadelphia Inquirer*, Tuesday, February 16, 1915, and Wednesday, February 17, 1915.

[110]Mount Moriah Cemetery Database, Genealogical Society of Pennsylvania, 2207 Chestnut Street, Philadelphia, Pennsylvania 19103 says SCHMIDT, Leonard 1915 Feb 18 Section 150, Lot 197.

[111]Mount Moriah Cemetery Database, Genealogical Society of Pennsylvania, 2207 Chestnut Street, Philadelphia, Pennsylvania 19103, also includes his father, Ernest Schmidt (1936), and at least 3 of his siblings Leona Schmidt (1956), Agnes C. Schmidt (1910), and Frieda

The couple had only one child, a daughter named Martha Schmidt/Smith. She married Joseph William Hassell and they had a son named Joseph William Hassell, Jr.

MARRIAGE TO JOHN J. ROE. The second marriage of Lydia E. Chambers was to John J. Roe. They were married on September 12, 1916.[114] At the time of their marriage both parties indicated they were living at 1333 South Corlies Street in the Grays Ferry section of South Philadelphia. They were still living at the same location in 1920.[115] The couple does not appear to have had any children. John J. Roe died on October 15, 1929, of sarcoma of the lung. He was buried in Holy Sepulchre Cemetery.[116]

Clark (1969) as well as her husband, Willard J. Clark (1969). Also, Death Certificate for Ernest Schmidt, April 11, 1907, Philadelphia City Archives, Philadelphia, Pennsylvania, FHL Microfilm Roll 1402878 which says: Ernest Schmidt, 1308 South 33rd Street, born: 1882 in Germany, died: 11 Apr 1907 in Philadelphia, aged: 24 years 4 months, buried: 14 Apr 1907 at Mount Moriah Cemetery. Also, Pennsylvania and New Jersey, Church and Town Records, 1708-1985, Historical Society of Pennsylvania, Mount Moriah Interment Records, Interment # 80380, Schmidt, Ernest, 24 yrs, April 14, 1907, Section 150, Lot 197.

[112]Pennsylvania and New Jersey, Church and Town Records, 1708-1985, Historical Society of Pennsylvania, Mount Moriah Interment Records, Interment # 123238, Schmidt, Caroline, 97 yrs, September 19, 1952, Section 150, Lot 197.

[113]Obituary, *Philadelphia Inquirer*, Saturday, April 9, 1910, says:

> SCHMIDT. On April 6, 1910, Agnes C., daughter of Ernest and Caroline Schmidt, in her 29th year. The relatives and friends are invited to attend the funeral services, on Sunday afternoon, at 2 o'clock, at her parents' residence, 2811 Wharton st. Interment at Mount Moriah.

[114]Affidavit of Applicant for Marriage License # 350776, September 11, 1916, (John J. Roe & Lydie (sic) C. Smith), City of Philadelphia, Philadelphia City Archives, Philadelphia, Pennsylvania, FHL Microfilm Roll 4120858. The application states that John J. Roe was born May 1, 1870 in New York, he was the son of Frank and Delia D. (Murphy) Roe, both deceased; and he was working as a store house manager. The application also indicates that Lydia C. Smith was born on February 27, 1872 in Philadelphia; she was the daughter of George and Anna (sic); her mother's maiden name was Chambers (sic); and she was never (sic) previously married.

[115]1920 U.S. Census (population), Pennsylvania, Philadelphia County, City of Philadelphia, Ward 36, E.D. 1289, page 2B, line 72, National Archives Microfilm Publication T625, Roll 1638, John J. Roe, 1333 Corlies Street.

[116]Death Certificate for John J. Roe, October 15, 1929, # 97053 & # 21292, Pennsylvania Division of Vital Statistics, New Castle, Pennsylvania.

WIDOWHOOD. After the death of her second husband, Lydia E. (Chambers) Schmidt/Smith Roe and her daughter, Martha (Schmidt/Smith) Hassell, and her family all lived together at 1333 South Corlies Street.[117,118] Tragically, Martha's husband, Joseph William Hassell, died from advanced tuberculosis on April 27, 1940, when he was 27 years old. He was buried at Mount Moriah Cemetery.[119] Their son, Joseph, Jr., was only 4 years old when his father died.

Undoubtedly, the emotional impact on the family was devastating. So was the financial impact. Both women went to work. According to Lydia's grand-nephew, Joseph D. Chambers, Aunt Lydie worked as a cashier at a movie theater on Woodland Avenue in West Philadelphia known as the Lindie.[120,121] According to Lydia's grand-niece, Josephine (Thompson) Marshall, during the 1930s, she and Lydia's daughter, Martha, worked together in the same office of an insurance company in Philadelphia.[122]

THE LATER YEARS. Lydia E. (Chambers) Schmidt/Smith Roe died on February 19, 1949, from a heart attack. She was buried in Mount Moriah Cemetery.[123] Her daughter, Martha (Schmidt/Smith) Hassell, died on August 5, 1990.[124] Martha's obituary read as follows:

---

[117]1930 U.S. Census (population), Pennsylvania, Philadelphia County, City of Philadelphia, Ward 36, E.D. 0140, page 20B, line 61, National Archives Microfilm Publication T626, Roll 2124, Lydia H. Roe, 1333 Corlies Street.

[118]1940 U.S. Census (population), Pennsylvania, Philadelphia County, City of Philadelphia, Ward 36, E.D. 51-1352, page 14B, line 64, National Archives Microfilm Publication T627, Roll 3730, Lydia Roe, 1333 Corlies Street.

[119]Death Certificate for Joseph Hassel (sic), April 27, 1940, # 34013 & # 9604, Pennsylvania Division of Vital Statistics, New Castle, Pennsylvania.

[120]Conversation on March 21, 1999, with the late Joseph D. Chambers, Claymont, Delaware, great- grandson of George Washington Chambers.

[121]Death Certificate for Lydia Chambers Roe, February 19, 1929, # 17822 & # 3642, Pennsylvania Division of Vital Statistics, New Castle, Pennsylvania says theater porter.

[122]Conversation on November 29, 1996, with the late Josephine Thompson Marshall, 121 Reillywood Avenue, Haddonfield, New Jersey 08033, great-granddaughter of George Washington Chambers.

[123]Death Certificate for Lydia Chambers Roe, February 19, 1949, # 17822 & # 3642, Pennsylvania Division of Vital Statistics, New Castle, Pennsylvania.

[124]Social Security Death Index, Martha Hassell, 163-03-9736, b. 16 Oct 1910, d. 5 Aug 1990. State SSN issued; Pennsylvania.

HASSELL, Suddenly, Aug 5 1990, MARTHA S. (nee Schmidt), beloved wife of the late Joseph Hassell Sr., grandmother of Joseph W. Hassell, Robert and Christopher Wetzler, mother-in-law of Mrs. Frances M. Wetzler. Relatives and friends are invited to her Viewing and Funeral Thurs. morn. after 8:30 A.M. Int. Mt. Moriah Cem. Donations in her memory to The American Diabetes Assoc. 100 N 17th St Phila. Pa 19103 would be appreciated.[125]

For some unexplained reason, Martha's son, Joseph William Hassell, Jr., was not mentioned in his mother's obituary. He died on September 26, 2006.[126] His obituary read as follows:

HASSELL, JOSEPH W., JR., on Sept 29, 2006, age 71. Services and interment private. RUFFENACH. F.H. 215-389-0876.[127]

According to the obituary of Martha (Schmidt/Smith) Hassell, her son, Joseph William Hassell, Jr., had at least one child, a son named Joseph W. Hassell.

Emma C. Chambers

Emma C. Chambers was born on March 23, 1875.[128] Undoubtedly, she was named after George Washington Chambers' sister, Emma (Chambers) Clark. Emma C. Chambers was known to everyone as Emmie or Aunt Emmie to her nieces and nephews.

MARRIAGE TO WILLIAM YOUNG SPENCE. She married William Young Spence on March 20, 1899, in Delaware County, Pennsylvania.[129] The Rev. J.N. Butler officiated. The

---

[125]Obituary, *Philadelphia Inquirer*, Wednesday, August 7, 1990, p. 4-B.

[126]Social Security Application and Claim Index, Joseph William Hassell, b. 22 Jun 1935 in Philadelphia, Pennsylvania, Father's Name: Joseph W. Hassell, Mother's Name: Martha Smith, d. 29 Sep 2006, Type of Claim: Original SSN. Notes: May 1950: Name listed as JOSEPH WILLIAM HASSELL; 07 Oct 2006: Name listed as JOSEPH W HASSELL.

[127]Obituary, *Philadelphia Inquirer*, Wednesday, October 4, 2006. NOTE: According to Ruffenbach Funeral Home the remains of Joseph W. Hassell, Jr., were cremated on October 3, 2006, and released to his step-brother, Edward Urban, who was in charge of the arrangements.

[128]George Chambers and Annie A. Chambers, widow, Civil War Pension Application SO 1304127, SC 1102701, WO 849418, WC 612527, Records of the Veterans Administration, Record Group 15, National Archives, Washington, D.C.

[129]Marriage Dockets, Volumes M-N, 1895 - 1900, Delaware County Courthouse, Delaware County, Pennsylvania, FHL Microfilm Roll 930559, says:

marriage was his second and her first.[130,131]

MARRIED LIFE TOGETHER. William Young Spence was born in Scotland and immigrated to the United States in 1875 or 1876 when he was about five years old. He was a naturalized American citizen. For many years, he worked as a bricklayer to support his family as well as various members of his wife's extended family.

It all began in 1899 after William Young Spence and Emma C. Chambers were married and the couple moved in with her parents and siblings at 3223 Lombard Street. It was there that the family was enumerated in 1900 as follows:

3223 LOMBARD STREET, WEST PHILADELPHIA

Chambers, George	Head W M Feb 1845 55 Married b. PA Stevedore
-, Annie	Wife W F Feb 1848 52 Married b. Scotland
-, Lydia	Daughter W F Feb 1874 26 Single b. PA Dressmaking
-, Annie A.	Daughter W F Feb 1879 21 Single b. PA Child Nurse
-, George	Son W M Jul 1881 18 Single b. PA Laborer
-, Bessie	Daughter W F Sep 1884 15 Single b. PA Saleswoman
Spence, William Y.	Head W M Feb 1870 30 Married b. Scotland Bricklayer
-, Emma C.	Wife W F Mar 1876 24 Married b. PA
-, Pauline L.	Daughter W F Jul 1899 10m Single b. PA[132]

William Y. Spence Born in Scotland 9th day of February A.D. 1870 Residing at Philada (sic) Bricklayer Occupation not Related by blood or marriage to the person whom he desires to marry was Married before and marriage was dissolved by death. Emma C. Chambers Born Philada (sic) on the 23rd day of March A.D. 1875 Residing at Philada (sic) Candymaker Occupation not Married before. 1899-3-20 Marriage License issued. 1899-3-23 Duplicate Certificate returned by Rev. J.N. Butler.

[130]Obituary, *Philadelphia Inquirer*, Friday, March 5, 1897, Saturday, March 6, 1897, and Sunday, March 7, 1897, says:

SPENCE - On March 4, Mamie M. wife of William Spence and daughter of George and Annie Moore, in her 22nd year. A patient sufferer at rest. The relatives and friends of the family are respectfully invited to attend the funeral on Sunday at 1 o'clock from her parents' residence, No. 1247 Patton street. Interment Fernwood Cemetery.

[131]Return of a Death in the City of Philadelphia, Mamie Spence, March 4, 1897, 1247 Patton Street, Ward 36, Philadelphia City Archives, Philadelphia, Pennsylvania 19108 says she died of pulmonary tuberculosis.

[132]1900 U.S. Census (population), Pennsylvania, Philadelphia County, City of Philadelphia, Ward 27, E.D. 659, page 13A, line 7, National Archives Microfilm Publications T623, Roll 1469.

Over the next ten years, the composition of the family changed somewhat. William Young Spence became the head of the household after George Washington Chambers died in 1906. Then, George Edwards Chambers and Lydia E. Chambers moved out after they married in 1905 and 1909, respectively. In 1910, those still living together at the Spence home were enumerated at 2823 Wharton Street as follows:

2823 WHARTON STREET , SOUTH PHILADELPHIA

Spence, William Y.	Head M W 40 Married b. Scotland Bricklayer at Contracting Firm
-, Emma C.	Wife F W 35 Married b. PA
-, Pauline L.	Daughter F W 10 Single b. PA
-. Leteta (sic) V.	Daughter F W 7 Single b. PA
-, William Y., Jr.	Son M W 5 Single b. PA
-, George E.	Son M W 1 Single b. PA
Chambers, Anna A.	MIL F W 63 Widow b. Scotland
-, Annie I.	SIL F W 32 Single b. PA Housekeeper at Home
McManus, Elizabeth H.	SIL F W 26 Married b. PA Forelady at Factory[133]

In 1911, Elizabeth H. (Chambers) McManus died at the Spence home from tuberculosis. Then, around 1917, William Young Spence appears to have moved the rest of the family, briefly, to 2417 South 61st Street.[134] After that, they all moved to 2235 68th Street where they were enumerated in 1920 as follows:

2235 68th STREET, WEST PHILADELPHIA

Spence, William Y.	Head M W 49 Married b. Scotland Bricklayer Construction
-, Emma	Wife F W 44 Married b. PA
-, Lydia	Daughter F W 17 Single b. PA Clerk Telephone Company
-, William, Jr.	Son M W 15 Single b. PA
-, George E.	Son M W 11 Single b. PA
Gurk, William F.	Head M W 22 Married b. PA Foreman Barrel Factory
-, Pauline L.	Wife F W 20 Married b. PA
-, William, Jr.	Son M W 10m Single b. PA
Chambers, Anna A.	MIL F W 72 Widow b Scotland
-, Anna I.	SIL F W 40 Single b PA[135]

Sometime after 1920, William Young Spence moved the family to 7119 Upland Street

---

[133]1910 U.S. Census (population), Pennsylvania, Philadelphia County, City of Philadelphia, Ward 36, E.D. 899, page 5A, line 12, Family Number 82, National Archives Microfilm Publication T624, Roll 1407.

[134]1917 Philadelphia City Directory.

[135]1920 U.S. Census (population), Pennsylvania, Philadelphia County, City of Philadelphia, Ward 40, E.D. 1490, page 6A, line 31, National Archives Microfilm Publication T625, Roll 1641.

where he rented a semi-detached, three story house on a 25 by 130 foot lot.[136] The house must have been quite satisfactory to everyone's needs because that is where they lived for the rest of their lives.[137,138]

DEATH OF ANNIE ADAM (EDWARDS) CHAMBERS. Annie Adam (Edwards) Chambers, widow of George Washington Chambers, died at the Spence home on December 27, 1927.[139] She was 80 years old. She was survived by two sons, William Scott Chambers and George E. Chambers, three daughters, Lydia E. (Chambers) Schmidt/Smith Roe, Emma (Chambers) Spence, and Annie I. Chambers, seven grandchildren, and four great-grandchildren. Her funeral services were held at the Spence home. She was laid out in the parlor. In fact, according to family legend, while all the adults gathered in the front parlor to mourn her passing, at least half a dozen or so of her grandchildren and great-grandchildren jumped up and down on the beds in one of the upstairs bedrooms.[140,141]

DEATH OF WILLIAM YOUNG SPENCE. After many years of hard work in support of his family, William Young Spence died at home on December 31, 1943, from influenza and edema

---

[136]Letter dated August 11, 2000, from Susan S. Koelble, Bareroots Research Services, Box 134, Southampton, Pennsylvania 18966-0134 transmitting a description of the property and copies of five deed transfers for 7119 Upland Street spanning the years 1891 to 1946 as contained in the Recorder of Deeds Registry Jacket, Philadelphia City Archives, Philadelphia, Pennsylvania.

[137]1930 U.S. Census (population), Pennsylvania, Philadelphia County, City of Philadelphia, Ward 40, E.D. 0228, page 13A, line 42, National Archives Microfilm Publication T626, Roll 2130 includes William Y. Spence (60), Emma R. Spence (54), William Y. Spence (25), George E. Spence (21), Anna Chambers (50) and 3 lodgers named Catherine Vile (13), George Schlater (12) and Henriette Schlater (10) .

[138]1940 U.S. Census (population), Pennsylvania, Philadelphia County, City of Philadelphia, Ward 40, E.D. 51-1612, page 13A, line 22, National Archives Microfilm Publication T627, Roll 3737 includes William Spence (70), Emma Spence (65), William Gurk (42), Pauline Gurk (40), William Gurk (21) and Anna Chambers (61).

[139]Death Certificate for Annie A. Chambers, December 27, 1927, # 110928 & # 26098, Pennsylvania Division of Vital Statistics, New Castle, Pennsylvania 16103.

[140]Conversation on July 31, 1995, with the late William Scott Chambers, 325 N.W. 95th Avenue, Plantation, FL 33324-7021.

[141]Kathryn Chambers Torpey, *The Edwards/Scott Family History*, (Alexandria, Virginia: Torpey Books, 2016), 30-35.

of the lungs.[142] The informant on his death certificate was his son, William Young Spence, Jr., of the same address. His obituary appeared in the *Philadelphia Inquirer* as follows:

> SPENCE, Dec. 31, William Y., husband of Emma C. Spence of 7119 Upland St. Relatives and friends invited to funeral Tues 1 PM from Yerkes Funeral Home 7031 Woodland Avenue. Int. Mt. Moriah Cem. Friends may call Mon. eve.[143,144]

WIDOWHOOD. Six days after Aunt Emmie was widowed, her sister, Annie I. Chambers, died at the Spence home from myocarditis and pleurisy.[145,146] The loss of both her husband and her sister in such a short period of time must have been draining. There is no doubt that the Spence home would have seemed eerily quiet. In her grief, Emma (Chambers) Spence would have needed to develop new routines and interests. Eventually she seems to have recovered. She continued living at 7119 Upland Street. Finally, on April 26, 1947, her daughter and son-in-law, William F. and Pauline (Spence) Gurk, bought the house from its owner, Sarah A. Gesner.[147] As Aunt Emmie got older, two of her grand-nephews, George Richards Chambers, Jr., and his brother, Joseph D. Chambers, remember cleaning her house on a regular basis in order to help out, but eventually they, as well as her other nieces and nephews, seem to have lost touch with Aunt Emmie and her family.[148]

THE DEATH OF EMMA (CHAMBERS) SPENCE. Emma C. (Chambers) Spence died on

---

[142]Death Certificate for William Y. Spence, December 31, 1943, # 118221 & # 28244, Pennsylvania Division of Vital Statistics, New Castle, Pennsylvania 16103.

[143]Obituary, *Philadelphia Inquirer*, Sunday, January 2, 1944, p. S-11.

[144]Letter dated May 25, 2000, from Susan S. Koelble, Bareroots Research Services, Box 134, Southampton, Pennsylvania 18966-0134 says there is no record of a will or intestate papers being filed on behalf of the estate of William Young Spence in the City of Philadelphia.

[145]Death Certificate for Annie I. Chambers, January 6, 1944, # 10155 & # 726, Pennsylvania Division of Vital Statistics, New Castle, Pennsylvania 16103.

[146]Obituary, *Philadelphia Inquirer*, Sunday, January 9, 1944, p. 8-S.

[147]Letter dated August 11, 2000, from Susan S. Koelble, Bareroots Research Services, Box 134, Southampton, Pennsylvania 18966-0134 transmitting copies of five deed transfers for 7119 Upland Street spanning the years 1891 to 1946 as contained in the Recorder of Deeds Registry Jacket, Philadelphia City Archives, Philadelphia, Pennsylvania.

[148]Conversation on March 21, 1999, with George R. Chambers, Jr., 618 Wilder Road, Wallingford, Pennsylvania 19806-6837 and the late Joseph D. Chambers, Claymont, Delaware, great-grandsons of George Washington Chambers.

October 4, 1960, from a coronary occlusion.[149] She was 85 years old at the time she died. She was predeceased by her son, William Young Spence, Jr., and her daughter, Pauline (Spence) Gurk. Although the death certificate says her usual place of residence was 7119 Upland Street in Philadelphia, her place of death is listed as 22 Mulberry Lane, Newtown Square, Delaware County, Pennsylvania. The informant was George Enge, her son-in-law, the husband of her daughter, Lydia Viola Spence.

Aunt Emmie's obituary appeared in the *Philadelphia Inquirer* as follows:

> SPENCE, On October 4 of 7119 Upland St., Emma C. (nee Chambers), wife of the late William Y. Relatives and friends are invited to funeral Sat., 10 AM from the Yerkes Funeral Home, 7031 Woodland Avenue. Int. Mt. Moriah Cem. Visiting Friday eve. [150]

Emma C. (Chambers) Spence was buried in Mount Moriah Cemetery on October 8, 1960, alongside her husband, William Young Spence.[151,152] No will or intestate papers were filed on behalf of her estate in the City of Philadelphia. In 1962, William F. Gurk and his second wife, Margaret, sold 7119 Upland Street.[153,154]

All efforts, to date, to trace the descendants of Aunt Emmie's children have resulted in failure.

---

[149]Death Certificate for Emma C. Spence, October 4, 1960, # 093397-60, Pennsylvania Division of Vital Statistics, New Castle, Pennsylvania 16103.

[150]Obituary, *Philadelphia Inquirer*, Friday, October 7, 1960, p. 52.

[151]Mount Moriah Register of Interments, William Y. Spence, # 118695, 73 years, January 4, 1944 and Emma Spence, # 126462, 85 years, October 8, 1960, Section 148, Lot 176/178, Genealogical Society of Pennsylvania, Philadelphia, Pennsylvania, Microfilm Roll XX 826:3.

[152]Mount Moriah Cemetery On-line Database, Genealogical Society of Pennsylvania, Philadelphia, Pennsylvania, <<https://genpa.org/>>, downloaded July 29, 2016. Note: They seem to have been buried in a plot belonging to the family of William Young Spence.

[153]Letter dated May 25, 2000, from Susan S. Koelble, Bareroots Research Services, Box 134, Southampton, Pennsylvania 18966-0134. Note: William Gurk remarried after the death of his first wife, Pauline L. (Spence) Gurk.

[154]Letter dated August 11, 2000, from Susan S. Koelble, Bareroots Research Services, Box 134, Southampton, Pennsylvania 18966-0134 transmitting a description of the property and copies of five deed transfers for 7119 Upland Street spanning the years 1891 to 1946 as contained in the Recorder of Deeds Registry Jacket, Philadelphia City Archives, Philadelphia, Pennsylvania.

Annie I. Chambers

Annie I. Chambers was born in Philadelphia on February 12, 1878.[155] She was probably named after her mother, Annie Adam (Edwards) Chambers. Assuming that her middle name might have been Isabella, she may also have been named after her maternal grandmother, Isabella (Scott) Edwards.

Annie I. Chambers never married. She lived with her older sister, Emma (Chambers) Spence, and worked periodically as a child nurse or as a housekeeper. She died January 6, 1944, at the Spence home from myocarditis and pleurisy.[156] Her obituary appeared in the *Philadelphia Inquirer* as follows:

> CHAMBERS - January 6, Anna I. sister of Emma C. Spence of 7119 Upland
> Street. Services Monday 1 PM Yerkes Funeral Home 7031 Woodland Avenue.
> Interment Mt. Moriah Cemetery. Friends may call Sunday evening.[157]

She was buried on January 10, 1944, in the Chambers family plot alongside her father, George Washington Chambers, her mother, Annie Adam (Edwards) Chambers, her baby sister, Eliza Jane Chambers, and her youngest sister, Elizabeth (Chambers) McManus.[158]

Elizabeth H. Chambers

Elizabeth H. Chambers was the youngest child of George Washington Chambers and Annie Adam (Edwards) Chambers. She was known to her friends and family as Bessie. She was born September 1, 1883, in Philadelphia.[159] She was probably named after George Washington Chambers' mother.

---

[155]George Chambers and Annie A. Chambers, widow, Civil War Pension Application SO 1304127, SC 1102701, WO 849418, WC 612527, Records of the Veterans Administration, Record Group 15, National Archives, Washington, D.C.

[156]Death Certificate for Annie I. Chambers, January 6, 1944, # 10155 & # 726, Pennsylvania Division of Vital Statistics, New Castle, Pennsylvania 16103 says February 12, 1880 (sic).

[157]Obituary, *Philadelphia Inquirer*, Sunday, January 9, 1944, p. 8-S.

[158]Letter dated July 20, 1995, from Lydia M. Jones, Director, Mt. Moriah Cemetery concerning the plot owned by George W. Chambers (Section 204, Lot 503).

[159]Record of Birth of Elizabeth Chambers, September 1, 1883, Book 1883, p. 332, Philadelphia City Archives, Philadelphia, Pennsylvania, Philadelphia City Births, 1860-1906, FHL Microfilm Roll 1289322 says: father George W. Chambers; mother Anna A.

She married Joseph W. McManus on April 16, 1907, at St. Agatha Roman Catholic Church located at 38th and Spring Garden Streets. At the time they applied for their marriage license, he was living at 3717 Aspen Street near the Philadelphia Zoo and she was living with her family at 3223 Lombard Street. Both addresses are in West Philadelphia.[160]

According to their marriage license application, Joseph W. McManus was born in Ireland on September 17, 1882. The application also says he was working as a fireman for the Pennsylvania Railroad.[161] He may have met Bessie through her brothers, William Scott Chambers and George Edwards Chambers, who worked for the B&O Railroad and the Pennsylvania Railroad, respectively.

The couple appears to have separated by 1910. Bessie (Chambers) McManus was living with her sister, Emma (Chambers) Spence, at 2823 Wharton Street.[162] Joseph W. McManus was living with his brother, John J. McManus, at 632 Union Place and working as a conductor for the transit company.[163] Joseph W. McManus died on October 8, 1918, of lobar pneumonia, a form of pneumonia that affects a large and continuous area of the lobe of a lung. At the time of his death, he was working as a brakeman. He was buried at Holy Cross Cemetery.[164]

From the time Bessie was fifteen onward, she worked variously as a saleswoman, a

---

[160]M. Laffitte Vieira, compiler, *West Philadelphia Illustrated: Early History of West Philadelphia and Its Environs; Its People and Its Historical Points*, (Philadelphia, Pennsylvania: Anvil Printing Company, 1903), 68, says St. Agatha Roman Catholic Church was established in 1865. In 1874, it moved to 38th and Spring Garden Streets in West Philadelphia.

[161]Affidavit of Applicant for Marriage License # 212231, April 16, 1907, (Joseph W. McManus & Elizabeth H. Chambers), City of Philadelphia, Philadelphia City Archives, Philadelphia, Pennsylvania.

[162]1910 U.S. Census (population), Pennsylvania, Philadelphia County, City of Philadelphia, Ward 36, E.D. 899, page 5A, line 12, Family Number 82, National Archives Microfilm Publication T624, Roll 1407.

[163]1910 U.S. Census (population), Pennsylvania, Philadelphia County, City of Philadelphia, Ward 24, E.D. 509, page 13A, line 11, Family Number 246, National Archives Microfilm Publication T624, Roll 1397.

[164]Death Certificate for Joseph McManus, October 8, 1918, # 147604 & # 28932, Pennsylvania Division of Vital Statistics, New Castle, Pennsylvania 16103. Also, Oliver Bair Funeral Home Record for Joseph McManus, October 15, 1918, Historical Society of Philadelphia, Philadelphia, Pennsylvania.

dressmaker, and as a forelady in a factory.[165] As best can be determined, she never had any children. She died at the age of twenty-six from tuberculosis which she may have contracted from her father, George Washington Chambers.[166] Her obituary appeared in the *Philadelphia Public Ledger* on Friday, January 20, 1911, as follows:

> McMANUS, On January 18, 1911, ELIZABETH McMANUS, daughter of
> Annie and the late George W. Chambers. The relatives and friends are invited to
> attend the funeral services on Sunday afternoon at 2 o'clock at the residence of
> her brother-in-law, William Spence, 2823 Wharton St. Interment Mt. Moriah.[167]

Elizabeth "Bessie" (Chambers) McManus was laid out on January 22, 1911, in a plush, crushed gray casket with a satin lining and silver handles. The plate inscription on her casket read: Elizabeth McManus, September 1, 1884 (sic) - January 18, 1911. The Reverend William Oxtoby of Tabernacle Presbyterian Church and the Reverend Oliphant Gibbons of Hope Presbyterian Church were asked to officiate at her funeral.[168]

She was buried in the Chambers family plot alongside her father, George Washington Chambers and her baby sister, Eliza Jane Chambers, both of whom predeceased her.[169] Her mother, Annie Adam (Edwards) Chambers, paid for her funeral. Unfortunately, due to a clerical error in the Mount Moriah Cemetery interment records, her name was mistakenly recorded as

---

[165]1900 U.S. Census (population), Pennsylvania, Philadelphia County, City of Philadelphia, Ward 27, E.D. 659, page 13A, line 7, National Archives Microfilm Publications T623, Roll 1469. Also, Affidavit of Applicant for Marriage License # 212231, April 16, 1907, (Joseph W. McManus & Elizabeth H. Chambers), City of Philadelphia, Philadelphia City Archives, Philadelphia, Pennsylvania. Also, 1910 U.S. Census (population), Pennsylvania, Philadelphia County, City of Philadelphia, Ward 36, E.D. 899, page 5A, line 12, Family Number 82, National Archives Microfilm Publication T624, Roll 1407.

[166]Death Certificate for Elizabeth McManus, January 18, 1911, # 5078 & # 1676, Pennsylvania Division of Vital Statistics, New Castle, Pennsylvania 16103 says she was born September 1, 1884 (sic).

[167]Obituary, *Philadelphia Public Ledger*, Friday, January 20, 1911, p. 18; Saturday, January 21, 1911, p. 7; and Sunday, January 22, 1911, p. 8.

[168]Oliver Bair Funeral Home Record for Elizabeth McManus, January 22, 1911, Historical Society of Philadelphia, Philadelphia, Pennsylvania.

[169]Letter dated July 20, 1995, from Lydia M. Jones, Director, Mt. Moriah Cemetery concerning the plot owned by George W. Chambers (Section 204, Lot 503).

"George W. Chambers."[170]

SONS OF GEORGE WASHINGTON CHAMBERS

George Washington Chambers and his wife, Annie Adam (Edwards) Chambers, had two sons - William Scott and George Edwards.

George Edwards Chambers

Their younger son, George Edwards Chambers, was born on July 1, 1880, in Philadelphia.[171] He may have been named after his father, George Washington Chambers, or his paternal grandfather, George Chambers, or his mother's oldest brother, George Edwards. According to family legend, he did not go too far in school, maybe only to the third grade, which was not uncommon in those days.[172]

MARRIAGE TO ANNIE RICHARDS. George Edwards Chambers and Annie Richards applied for a marriage license in Philadelphia on April 24, 1905, but there is no return on the marriage so the exact date and place of their marriage is unknown.[173] According to family legend, the Chambers and the Richards families were Protestant, possibly Methodist, so they may have been married at a local Methodist church.[174,175] To add to the mystery, their grandson, George R. Chambers, Jr., is in possession of a large oval wedding picture of his grandparents that

---

[170]Mount Moriah Register of Interments, George W. Chambers, # 85734, 26 years, January 22, 1911, Section 204, Lot 503, Genealogical Society of Pennsylvania, Philadelphia, Pennsylvania, Microfilm Roll XX 826:2.

[171]George Chambers and Annie A. Chambers, widow, Civil War Pension Application SO 1304127, SC 1102701, WO 849418, WC 612527, Records of the Veterans Administration, Record Group 15, National Archives, Washington, D.C.

[172]Conversation on March 21, 1999, with George R. Chambers, Jr., 63 Winona Avenue, Norwood, Pennsylvania 19074-1415.

[173]Affidavit of Applicant for Marriage License # 184963, April 24, 1905, (George E. Chambers, Jr. & Ann Richards), City of Philadelphia, Philadelphia City Archives, Philadelphia, Pennsylvania.

[174]Letter dated January 26, 1999 from the late Lois Chambers, 618 Wilder Road, Wallingford, Pennsylvania 19806-6837, wife of George R. Chambers, Jr.

[175]Conversation on March 21, 1999, with George R. Chambers, Jr., 63 Winona Avenue, Norwood, Pennsylvania 19074-1415.

contains a written notation on the back that says "Wilmington, Delaware."[176]

THE EARLY YEARS. When George Edwards Chambers and Annie Richards applied for their marriage license in Philadelphia on April 24, 1905, he listed his address as 3223 Lombard Street and she listed her address as 3233 Locust Street. Both of these addresses are in West Philadelphia. According to family legend, in the early years of their marriage they may have lived in the Grays Ferry section of South Philadelphia just above an area known as the Devil's Pocket which was then populated primarily by people of Irish, Welsh and Scots-Irish ancestry, but this information could not be verified.[177]

THEIR FIRST CHILD, ANNIE CHAMBERS. George Edwards and Annie (Richards) Chambers' first child was a baby girl named Annie Chambers who was still born at 5 A.M. on Monday, June 24, 1907, after a "difficult labour." Both the record of her birth and the record of her death indicate that Annie Chambers was still born at 3233 Locust Street, the home of her maternal grandparents, David and Susanna (Thomas) Richards. Annie (Richards) Chambers must have returned to her parents' home for the birth of her first child because the birth record states that the residence of the parents was Washington, D.C., where the father worked as a conductor for the railroad.[178,179]

According to the Oliver Bair Funeral Home records, Annie Chambers was buried at 3 P.M. on the same day she died.[180] After the family dressed the baby in her own little dress, she was carefully laid to rest in a tiny two-foot coffin with a satin lining which was placed inside a pine case. Then, she was buried in the Chambers family plot at Mount Moriah Cemetery alongside her paternal grandfather, George Washington Chambers, who had died a year earlier on

----

[176]The wedding picture of George Edwards Chambers and Annie Richards is in the possession of George R. Chambers, Jr., 63 Winona Avenue, Norwood, Pennsylvania 19074-1415.

[177]Conversation on March 21, 1999, with the late Joseph D. Chambers, Claymont, Delaware, great-grandson of George Washington Chambers.

[178]Record of Birth for Annie Chambers, stillborn, June 24, 1907, # 11371, Philadelphia City Archives, Philadelphia, Pennsylvania.

[179]Death Certificate for Annie Chambers, stillborn, June 24, 1907, # 16568, Philadelphia City Archives, Philadelphia, Pennsylvania.

[180]Oliver Bair Funeral Home Record for Annie Chambers, June 24, 1907, Historical Society of Philadelphia, Philadelphia, Pennsylvania.

May 9, 1906.[181] The bill for the funeral and the burial was paid in cash by Annie Adam (Edwards) Chambers, the baby's paternal grandmother.

THEIR SECOND CHILD, GEORGE RICHARDS CHAMBERS. George Edwards and Annie (Richards) Chambers' second child, George Richards Chambers, was born at 5:30 A.M. on Monday, September 14, 1908. According to the record of his birth, he was born at 3220 (sic) Locust Street; his parents were living at 3233 Locust Street; and his father was employed as a brakeman for the railroad.[182]

Sadly, their son was afflicted with infantile paralysis (i.e., poliomyelitis) which seriously damaged his left leg.[183] Reportedly, Annie (Richards) Chambers tried her best to amuse her son by settling him comfortably in a special chair that was high enough so the child could look out the front window of the family home and see what was going on around him in the neighborhood. The lifelong condition was debilitating and it thwarted George Richards Chambers' ambition to enlist in the U.S. Navy during World War II.[184]

After graduating from eighth grade, George Richards Chambers went to work repairing pumps for the Gould Pump Company at 111 N. 3rd Street. Later, he served an apprenticeship with Walter B. Smith at 807 S. Vodges Street and became a professional painter. During the early years of the Depression, he worked variously as a truck driver for the Railways Express Company at 18th and Market Streets and as a painter for Pat Patterson at 5150 Arch Street.

---

[181]Letter dated July 20, 1995, from Lydia M. Jones, Director, Mt. Moriah Cemetery concerning the plot owned by George W. Chambers (Section 204, Lot 503).

[182]Return of Birth for George Richards Chambers, September 14, 1908, # 11166, Philadelphia City Archives, Philadelphia, Pennsylvania.

[183]Eugene W. Jackson, Chairman, *Professional Guide to Diseases, Second Edition*, (Springhouse, Pennsylvania: Springhouse Corporation, 1987), 222, says that poliomyelitis is an acute communicable disease caused by the polio virus and ranges in severity from unapparent infection to fatal paralytic illness. First recognized in 1840, poliomyelitis became epidemic in Norway and Sweden in 1905. Outbreaks of the disease reached pandemic proportion in Europe, North America, Australia, and New Zealand during the first half of the 20th century where it struck most often during the summer and fall. At that time, it was confined mainly to infants and children. The disease peaked during the 1940's and the early 1950's and led to the development of the Salk vaccine, rightly considered one of the miracle drugs of modern medicine.

[184]Conversation on March 21, 1999, with George R. Chambers, Jr., 63 Winona Avenue, Norwood, Pennsylvania 19074-1415 re: family story Gertrude (Richards) Knitter, sister of Annie (Richards) Chambers, once told her niece and namesake, Gertrude (Flenard) D'Andrea.

In 1934, George Richards Chambers married Mary Luciano.[185] In order to support his wife and growing family, he took a job as a shop foreman for Frank O'Hannlon at 61 N. 62nd Street where he supervised five painters. After the death of his father, he moved his family including his mother to Primos, Delaware County, Pennsylvania where he rented a small farm at Cook and Garfield Avenue.[186] There, he raised chickens, ducks, and goats and went into the business of selling eggs. Later, he took a job in a steel mill in Eddystone, Delaware County, Pennsylvania where he worked until he retired. In his spare time, he enjoyed building model ships.[187]

THEIR THIRD CHILD, GERTRUDE HELEN CHAMBERS. George Edwards and Annie (Richards) Chambers' third child was a little girl named Gertrude Helen Chambers. She was named after her maternal aunt, Gertrude (Richards) Knitter, sister of Annie (Richards) Chambers.[188] Sadly, she died from malnutrition and exhaustion on March 18, 1911, in Washington D.C., when she was 3 months old. She was buried in Woodlawn Cemetery in Washington, D.C.[189,190]

---

[185]Marriage License Index, George R. Chambers & Mary Luciano, 1934, # 633182, City of Philadelphia, Philadelphia City Archives, Philadelphia, Pennsylvania.

[186]The Worker's Employment History Form for George Richards Chambers, dated July 23, 1940, Federal Works Agency, Work Projects Administration for Pennsylvania, is in the possession of George R. Chambers, Jr., 63 Winona Avenue, Norwood, Pennsylvania 19074-1415.

[187]Conversation on March 21, 1999, with George R. Chambers, Jr., 63 Winona Avenue, Norwood, Pennsylvania 19074-1415.

[188]Gertrude (Richards) Knitter was an older sister of Annie (Richards) Chambers. Apparently, the two sisters must have been especially close because Gertrude is buried beside her sister, Annie, in Arlington Cemetery. Her headstone reads:

KNITTER
MY BELOVED SISTER
GERTRUDE H.
1881 - 1939

[189]Death Certificate for Gertrude Helen Chambers, March 18, 1911, # 197819, Washington, D.C., District of Columbia Death Records, <<www.ancestry.com>>, downloaded July 29, 2015. Note: The baby may have died of marasmus, a progressive wasting of the body, occurring chiefly in young children and associated with insufficient intake or malabsorption of food.

[190]Deaths Reported, *The Sunday Star*, Sunday, March 19, 1911, Part 1, p. 2 says:

WORKING AS A BRAKEMAN. According to family legend, George Edwards Chambers worked as a brakeman for the Pennsylvania Railroad.[191] During that time, he and his family lived at the following locations:

1905	3223 Lombard Street, laborer	Philadelphia City Directory
1906	3223 Lombard Street, brakeman	Philadelphia City Directory
1906	526 1st Street, S.E., brakeman	Washington, D.C. City Directory
1907	402 South Capitol Street, brakeman	Washington, D.C. City Directory
1907	Washington, D.C., conductor	Birth Certificate of Annie Chambers[192]
1908	146 Heckman Street, S.E., brakeman	Washington, D.C. City Directory
1908	3233 Locust Street, brakeman	Birth Certificate of George R. Chambers[193]
1910	503 G Street, S.E., brakeman	1910 U.S. Census, Washington, D.C.[194]
1910	313 C Street, S.E., brakeman	Washington, D.C. City Directory
1911	110 Heckman Street, S.E., brakeman	Washington, D.C. City Directory
1911	110 Heckman Street, S.E.	Death Certificate of Gertrude H. Chambers
1912	123 N. 57th Street, brakeman (inconclusive)	Philadelphia City Directory
1912	832 E 17th, engr (inconclusive)	Wilmington City Directory [195]
1913	2235 Pine Street, brakeman	Wilmington City Directory
1916	2235 Pine Street, brakeman	Wilmington City Directory

On the railroad, the conductor and the brakeman were in charge of the train. They usually rode in the caboose while the train was underway. This is in contrast to the engineer and the firemen who rode in the cab of the engine and never left the cab except in an emergency to inspect or possibly work on the engine.

The conductor was responsible for dealing with the railroad clerks and for maintaining all the records concerning which freight cars were to be dropped off or picked up at the warehouses or yards along the route. The brakeman was responsible for coordinating the schedule with the conductor and hooking up the freight cars and releasing them at the time of delivery. The brakeman was also responsible for inspecting the train from the cupola in the caboose while the

---

Gertrude H. Chambers, 3 months, 110 Heckman street, southeast.

[191]Conversation on March 21, 1999, with George R. Chambers, Jr., 63 Winona Avenue, Norwood, Pennsylvania 19074-1415.

[192]Record of Birth for Annie Chambers, stillborn, June 24, 1907, # 11371, Philadelphia City Archives, Philadelphia, Pennsylvania.

[193]Return of Birth for George Richards Chambers, September 14, 1908, # 11166, Philadelphia City Archives, Philadelphia, Pennsylvania.

[194]1910 U.S. Census (population), Washington, District of Columbia, Precinct 5, E.D. 94, page 5A, line 38, Family Number 105, National Archives Microfilm Publication T624, Roll 151.

[195]1912 Wilmington City Directory says: Chambers, George (Anna) engr 832 E 17th

train was underway and operating the hand brakes. In fact, before the advent of air brakes, the brakeman was frequently seen walking along the top of the freight cars and applying and releasing the mechanical brakes on each freight car whenever the engineer "whistled" for brakes. After the invention of air brakes, the brakeman was also responsible for connecting and testing the air breaks on each freight car which were then controlled by the engineer from the locomotive.[196],[197.]

Definitely a tough job for a strong man with no fear of heights.

WAR WORK. Beginning in 1917, it appears that George Edwards Chambers worked as a millwright for the E.I. DuPont Company where he was engaged in the manufacture of smokeless gun powder. During that time, the Chambers family lived at the following address:

1917	603 E. 22nd Street, laborer	Wilmington City Directory
1918	603 E. 22nd Street, millwright	WW I Draft Registration Card[198]
1919	603 E. 22nd Street, millwright	Wilmington City Directory

During World War I, the DuPont powder works were located in Wilmington, Delaware, and at Carney's Point, New Jersey. A great deal of men were employed in these "graining mills" during World War I where they were responsible for cracking large lumps of gun powder into smaller grains of various desired sizes for the production of the finished product - munitions. During the war years (1914 - 1918), the E.I. DuPont Company grew to an enormous size and became of indescribable importance to the nation and its allies in winning the war.[199]

Admittedly, this record of employment is inconsistent with family legend that George Edwards Chambers always worked for the railroad while the family lived in Wilmington (and possibly in Baltimore).[200] Nevertheless, it appears to be accurate and may have been necessary in order for George Edwards Chambers to be at home more often to help his wife with their son

---

[196]E-mail dated April 23, 2000, from the late William Scott Chambers, 325 N.W. 95th Avenue, Plantation, FL 33324-7021.

[197]A Brakemen's Job, <<http://www.info200.net/~petegrk/brakemen.html>>, downloaded April 25, 2000.

[198]World War I Draft Registration Card for George Edward Chambers, September 13, 1918, Wilmington, Delaware, FHL Microfilm Roll 1570710. Whether he served in World War I is unknown.

[199]Wilson Lloyd Bevan, PhD, editor, *History of Delaware - Past and Present*, 4 volumes (New York: Lewis Historical Publishing Company, Inc., 1929), v. 2, 831.

[200]Conversation on March 21, 1999, with George R. Chambers, Jr., 63 Winona Avenue, Norwood, Pennsylvania 19074-1415.

who was seriously ill with infantile paralysis.

THE LATER YEARS. The family appears to have returned to Philadelphia in 1919. Their address at that time was as follows:

1919	143 N. Wanamaker Street, ship worker	Philadelphia City Directory
1920	143 N. Wanamaker Street, reamer/shipyard	1920 U.S. Census, Philadelphia, PA
1921/22	143 N. Wanamaker, ship worker	Philadelphia City Directory

In 1920 census, George Edwards Chambers and his family were enumerated as follows:

143 N. WANAMAKER STREET, WEST PHILADELPHIA

Chambers, George	Head M W 39 Married b. PA Reamer, Shipyard
-, Annie	Wife F W 39 Married b. PA
-, George R.	Son M W 11 Single b. PA
Richards, David P.	FIL M W 63 Widower b. PA Machinist Orphanage
Flenard, Charles W.	BIL M W 20 Married, b. PA Tank [–ester] Shipyard
-, Dorothy	SIL F W 17 Married b PA[201]

Apparently, George Edwards Chambers returned to work as a brakeman at some point after 1920. During that time, he and the family lived at the following address:

1923-27	225 N. Hobart, brakeman	Philadelphia City Directory

His grandson, George R. Chambers, Jr., remembers being told that his grandfather would frequently arrive home from work with large bags of oysters from the shore which the whole family would enjoy eating raw and washing down with beer. He also remembers being told that his grandfather belonged to the Brotherhood of Railway and Steamship Clerks, Freight Handlers, Express, and Station Employees, Victory Lodge 2151, and that he may also have been a Mason. Unfortunately, there is no official record of his work with the railroad on file with the Railroad Retirement Board because it all appears to have occurred prior to 1930.[202] There is also no record that he had an account with the Pennsylvania Railroad Company's Volunteer Relief Department which offered an insurance plan providing sick and death benefits for the worker and

---

[201]1920 U.S. Census (population), Pennsylvania, Philadelphia County, City of Philadelphia, Ward 34, E.D. 1190, page 13A, line 18, National Archives Microfilm Publication T625, Roll 1630.

[202]Letter dated April 20, 2000, from Bill Poulos, Director of Public Affairs, Railroad Retirement Board, 844 North Rush Street, Chicago, IL 60611-2092 states that George E. Chambers is not listed in their past service records which appears to indicate that all his actual railroad employment occurred before 1937.

his family.[203]

By 1930, George E. Chambers and his family were living at 36 South Salford Street. He was working as a filing clerk at an express company. The family was enumerated as follows:

36 SOUTH SALFORD STREET, WEST PHILADELPHIA

George E. Chambers   Head M W 49 Married b. PA Filing Clerk, Express Company
Anna Chambers   Wife W F 49 Married b. PA
George Chambers   Son W M 20 Single b. PA Chauffeur Truck
David P. Richards   FIL W M 74 Widower b. PA Watchman Building[204]

FAMILY GATHERINGS. Over the years, George Edwards Chambers made frequent trips with his wife, Annie (Richards) Chambers, to visit his brother, William Scott Chambers, and his wife, Josephine (Reitze) Chambers, at their home located at 5313 Yocum Street in West Philadelphia. According to family legend, everyone always had a good time at these family gatherings as Aunt Annie (Richards) Chambers was a delightful woman, short and somewhat stout, who had a great sense of humor. In fact, her grand-nephew, William Scott Chambers' most vivid recollection of Aunt Annie (Richards) Chambers is that she and Aunt Emmie (Chambers) Spence got along really well together. They were always laughing and entertained everyone present with their funny stories.[205]

DEATH OF GEORGE EDWARDS CHAMBERS. George Edwards Chambers died on June 26, 1937, at the age of 57 of hypertensive cardiovascular disease.[206] His obituary appeared in the *Philadelphia Inquirer* as follows:

CHAMBERS, June 27 (sic), George F. (sic), husband of Ann Chambers (nee Richards) formerly of 32nd and Locust Sts. Relatives and friends, also Brotherhood of Railway Clerks invited to funeral services Thurs., 2:30 P.M., late residence, 20 N. Dewey St. Int. Arlington Cem. Friends call Wed eve.[207]

---

[203]Pennsylvania Railroad Voluntary Relief Fund Records (MG 286), Pennsylvania State Archives, 350 North Street, Harrisburg, Pennsylvania 17120-0090.

[204]1930 U.S. Census (population), Pennsylvania, Philadelphia County, City of Philadelphia, Ward 46, E.D. 0509, page 8A, line 50, National Archives Microfilm Publication T626, Roll 2140.

[205]Conversation on July 31, 1995, with the late William Scott Chambers, 325 N.W. 95th Avenue, Plantation, FL 33324-7021.

[206]Death Certificate for George E. Chambers, June 26, 1937, # 56723 & # 13852, Pennsylvania Department of Vital Statistics, New Castle, Pennsylvania.

[207]Obituary, *Philadelphia Inquirer*, Wednesday, June 30, 1937, p. 35.

At the time of his death, George Edwards and Annie (Richards) Chambers, were living at 20 N. Dewey Street in Philadelphia and he was working as a platform man at the American Railway Express Company.[208] His grand-niece, Josephine (Thompson) Marshall, remembers attending her uncle's funeral and that it was an emotional scene at the cemetery where he was laid to rest. His daughter-in-law, Mary (Luciano) Chambers, with whom he must have been particularly close, was very distraught at his passing.[209] Undoubtedly, he was much loved by his family and remembered fondly by everyone who knew him.

After the death of George Edwards Chambers, his widow, Annie (Richards) Edwards continued living with her son and his wife, George Richards and Mary (Luciano) Chambers. She moved with them to Primos in Delaware County where she was enumerated with them in 1940 at 445 Cook Avenue, Darby Township, Delaware County, Pennsylvania.[210]

DEATH OF ANNIE (RICHARDS) CHAMBERS. Annie (Richards) Chambers died on January 17, 1953, at 6926 Chester Avenue in Philadelphia from pulmonary edema brought on by hypertensive cardiovascular disease.[211] She was 72 years old. Her obituary appeared in the *Philadelphia Inquirer* as follows:

> CHAMBERS, Jan, 17, 1953, ANNIE (nee Richards), widow of George, formerly of 33d (sic) and Locust Sts. Relatives and friends are invited to service Wed., 2 P.M., David [G.] Frankenfield Bldg., 317 N. 52d St. Int. Arlington Cem. Friends may call Tues. eve.[212]

---

[208]Death Certificate for George E. Chambers, June 26, 1937, # 56723 & # 13852, Pennsylvania Department of Vital Statistics, New Castle, Pennsylvania.

[209]E-mail dated March 5, 1999, from the late William Scott Chambers, 325 N.W. 95th Avenue, Plantation, FL 33324-7021.

[210]1940 U.S. Census (population), Pennsylvania, Delaware County, Darby Township, E.D. 23-68, page 7A, line 30, National Archives Microfilm Publication T627, Roll 3491.

George Chambers	Head 31 Married b. PA House Painting
Mary Chambers	Wife 22 Married b. PA
George Chambers	Son 5 Single b. PA
Dorothy Chambers	Daughter 4 Single b. PA
Joseph Chambers	Son 3 Single b. PA
Anna Chambers	Mother 59 Widow b. PA

[211]Death Certificate for Annie Chambers, January 17, 1953, # 1519 & # 6[9]01-461, Pennsylvania Department of Vital Statistics, New Castle, Pennsylvania.

[212]Obituary, *Philadelphia Inquirer*, Tuesday, January 20, 1953, p. 29.

ARLINGTON CEMETERY, DREXEL HILL. George E. and Annie (Richards) Chambers are buried together at Arlington Cemetery in Drexel Hill, Delaware County, Pennsylvania.[213] They are buried alongside their only surviving child, George Richards Chambers, who died on September 29, 1984, and his wife, Mary (Luciano) Chambers who predeceased him on January 24, 1979.[214, 215]

William Scott Chambers

William Scott Chambers, the older son of George Washington Chambers and Annie Adam (Edwards) Chambers was named after his mother's brother, William Scott Edwards.[216] He was born on June 5, 1867, in Philadelphia and he was baptized on January 12, 1868, at the Church of the Redemption, an Episcopal Church located at 22nd and Callowhill.[217,218] Not much is known about his childhood except that he claimed to have attended an Episcopal Church in the center of town (possibly the Church of the Redemption or Holy Trinity Episcopal) when he was a

---

[213]Burial Record, Arlington Cemetery, Lansdowne Avenue and School Lane, Drexel Hill, Pennsylvania 19026 concerning the plot owned by Anna and George R. Chambers (Lot 1499 Silverbrook Section).

[214]Obituary, *Philadelphia Inquirer*, Tuesday, October 2, 1984, p. 2-D.

> CHAMBERS, Sept, 29, 1984, of Phila., GEORGE R., SR., husband of the late Mary (nee Luciano), father of George R., Jr., Dorothy A. Brooks, and Joseph D., Sr., also survived by 14 grandchildren and 2 great grandchildren. Relatives and friends are invited to the funeral service, Wed. 2 P.M., at the MARVIL FUNERAL HOME, 1110 Main Street, Darby, where friends may call Wed. after 1 P.M. Int. Arlington Cem. In lieu of flowers, contributions in Mr. Chambers' memory to American Diabetes Assoc., 919 Walnut St., Phila., Pa, would be appreciated by the family.

[215]Obituary, *Philadelphia Inquirer*, Friday, January 26, 1979, p. 2-D.

> CHAMBERS, On Jan. 24, 1979, Mary (nee Luciano) of 6926 Chester Ave., beloved wife of George R. Chambers, Sr. Relatives and friends invited to funeral Sat., 10:30 A.M. at YERKES FUNERAL HOME, 7031 Woodland Ave., where friends may call Fri. eve. after 7. Int. Arlington Cem.

[216]Kathryn Chambers Torpey, *The Edwards/Scott Family History*, (Alexandria, Virginia: Torpey Books, 2016), 22-36.

[217]Birth Certificate for William Chambers, June 5, 1867, # 75994 & # 166686, City of Philadelphia, Department of Records, Vital Statistics, Philadelphia, Pennsylvania 19107.

[218]Church of the Redemption (Protestant Episcopal) Baptismal Register, Historical Society of Pennsylvania, Philadelphia, Pennsylvania.

youngster where he sung in the choir[219].

MARRIAGE TO SARAH (WHITE) KEENAN. The first wife of William Scott Chambers was Sarah (White) Keenan. They were married on February 1, 1894, at St. James Roman Catholic Church located at 38th and Chestnut Streets in West Philadelphia.[220,221] At the time they applied for their marriage license they were living across the street from each other in West Philadelphia. William Scott Chambers was living with his parents at 3211 St. James Street and Sarah (White) Keenan was living with her father, Richard White, at 3208 St. James Street. According to the application, Sarah (White) Keenan was a widow. She was previously married to William Keenan who died on April 30, 1890.[222,223]

From the time she was very young, Sarah (White) Keenan Chambers was known to her

---

[219]Conversation on April 14, 1997, with the late Josephine Thompson Marshall, 121 Reillywood Avenue, Haddonfield, New Jersey 08033.

[220]Affidavit of Applicant for Marriage License # 66279, January 22, 1894, (William Scott Chambers & Sarah Keenan), City of Philadelphia, Philadelphia City Archives, Philadelphia, Pennsylvania.

[221]M. Laffitte Vieira, compiler, *West Philadelphia Illustrated: Early History of West Philadelphia and Its Environs; Its People and Its Historical Points*, (Philadelphia, Pennsylvania: Anvil Printing Company, 1903), 62, says St. James Roman Catholic Church was established in 1850 at 38th and Chestnut Streets in West Philadelphia.

[222]Obituary, *Philadelphia Public Ledger*, Thursday, May 1, 1890, p. 4; Friday, May 2, 1890, p. 4; and Saturday, May 3, 1890, p. 4.

> KEENAN, On the 30th ult. William J. Keenan, aged 30 years.

> The relatives and friends of the family are respectfully invited to attend the funeral on Saturday morning at 8:30 o'clock from his late residence 3241 St. James Street. Solemn High Mass at St. James Church, Thirty-eighth and Chestnut Streets. To proceed to Old Cathedral Cemetery.

[223]Obituary, *Philadelphia Inquirer*, Friday, May 2, 1890, p. 5.

> KEENAN, On the 30th ult. William J. Keenan, aged 30 years.

friends and family as Sallie.[224,225] Her best friend was Elizabeth Reitze, the older sister of Josephine Irene Reitze who later became the second wife of William Scott Chambers.

Sadly, Sarah (White) Keenan Chambers died from tuberculosis (i.e, consumption) on August 14, 1894.[226] Her obituary appeared in the *Philadelphia Public Ledger* as follows:

> CHAMBERS - On the 14th inst., Sarah, wife of William Chambers and daughter of Richard White, aged 23 (sic).
>
> The relatives and friends of the family are respectfully invited to attend the funeral on Saturday morning at 7:30 o'clock from her late residence, 3237 Marston [later Lombard] street. Solemn High Mass at St. James Church, Thirty-eighth and Chestnut streets at 9 o'clock. Interment at Old Cathedral Cemetery.[227]

She was buried on August 18, 1894, alongside her first husband, William Keenan, in a plot belonging to her father, Richard White, at Old Cathedral Cemetery.[228] As best can be determined, she never had any children.[229]

MARRIAGE TO JOSEPHINE IRENE REITZE The second wife of William Scott Chambers

---

[224] 1870 U.S. Census (population), First Enumeration, Pennsylvania, Philadelphia County, City of Philadelphia, Ward 10, page 243B, National Archives Microfilm Publication M593, Roll 1395.

[225] 1880 U.S. Census (population), Pennsylvania, Philadelphia County, City of Philadelphia, Ward 27, E.D. 582, page 214C, sheet 27, line 49, National Archives Microfilm Publication T9, Roll 1186.

[226] 1894 Death Register, City of Philadelphia, # 3943, Sarah CHAMBERS, August 14, 1894, Philadelphia City Archives, Philadelphia, Pennsylvania

[227] Obituary, *Philadelphia Public Ledger*, Thursday, August 16, 1894, p. 6, and Friday, August 17, 1894, p. 6.

[228] Letter dated March 10, 1998, from Veronica T. Johnson, Assistant Director, Catholic Cemeteries Office, 111 South 38th Street, Philadelphia, Pennsylvania 19104- 3179 concerning the plot owned by Richard White (Section Q, Range 3, Lot 66).

[229] Letter dated September 30, 1997, from Christine Friend, Philadelphia Archdiocesan Historical Research Center, 100 East Wynnewood Road, Wynnewood, Pennsylvania 19096-3001.

was Josephine Irene Reitze, the daughter of Christopher Reitze and Lucy Devlin.[230,231] According to their marriage license, he was living at 3223 Marston [later Lombard] Street and she was living at 4230 Lancaster Avenue when they applied for their license. Both addresses are in West Philadelphia. They were married on March 30, 1896, at the Mantua Baptist Church located at Fairmount Avenue and N. 40th Street in West Philadelphia.[232,233,234] The Reverend Jacob G. Walker, Minister of the Gospel, officiated at the marriage ceremony.

MARRIED LIFE TOGETHER. From all accounts, the marriage of William Scott and Josephine (Reitze) Chambers was a happy one. William Scott Chambers was a handsome man, 6'1" with a typical Scottish look that he inherited from his mother. At the time they were married, he had a good job with the B&O Railroad where he was employed as a fireman. Later, he became an engineer. He was well paid, too, so he always gave his wife, Josephine, his weekly wages and kept his overtime pay for himself. For entertainment, the family went downtown together to shop at Wanamakers once a month. Sometimes, they would all go to a show, then to lunch, and then to another show.

According to family legend, William Scott Chambers' leisure time activities included acting and tap dancing.[235] His granddaughter, Josephine (Thompson) Marshall, recalls that when the big shows came to town, her grandfather was often an extra in the cast. In fact, according to his granddaughter, there was a small piece of hardwood floor between the kitchen and the dining

---

[230]1877 Birth Register, p. 181, (Josephine REIZ - July 4, 1877), City of Philadelphia, Philadelphia City Archives, Philadelphia, Pennsylvania.

[231]*Reitze Family Bible - Latin Vulgate Version*, (New York: 35 Gold Street, 1844) was in the possession of the late Josephine Thompson Marshall, 121 Reillywood Avenue, Haddonfield, New Jersey 08033-2201.

[232]Affidavit of Applicant for Marriage License # 84108, March 27, 1896, (William Scott Chambers & Josephine Irene Reitze), City of Philadelphia, Philadelphia City Archives, Philadelphia, Pennsylvania.

[233]The original marriage certificate for William Scott Chambers and Josephine I. Reitze was in the possession of the late William Scott Chambers, 325 N.W. 95th Avenue, Plantation, Florida 33324.

[234]M. Laffitte Vieira, compiler, *West Philadelphia Illustrated: Early History of West Philadelphia and Its Environs; Its People and Its Historical Points*, (Philadelphia, Pennsylvania: Anvil Printing Company, 1903), 68, says Mantua Baptist Church was established in 1872. The church was built in 1873 at Fortieth Street and Fairmount Avenue in West Philadelphia.

[235]Conversation on November 29, 1999, with the late Josephine Thompson Marshall, 121 Reillywood Avenue, Haddonfield, New Jersey 08033.

room of their home at 5313 Yocum Street in West Philadelphia on which her grandfather would almost invariably tap dance every time he crossed over it.

According to his great-grandson, David Harrington Marshall, Jr., William Scott Chambers (along with his brother-in-law, Chris Reitze, Jr.) also participated in gymnastics at Turners Hall located on the northeast corner of Board and Columbia Streets.[236] Turners Hall was built by the Philadelphia Turngemeinde, the local German sports organization. It was the scene of many sports events before the building was sold to Temple University in 1946. Those who exercised at Turners Hall were known as turnvereines. The turnvereine were dedicated to the principle of "a sound mind in a sound body," stressing gymnastics and other sports activities as well as encouraging singing and offering art and language classes. Thus, Turners Hall housed physical education activities, a community swimming pool, and art studios.[237]

MAKING A HOME. Their first child, Henry Grafe Chambers, was born on January 8, 1897, at 1232 South 34th Street in the Grays Ferry section of South Philadelphia. Their second child, Lucy Elizabeth Chambers, is believed to have been born there too on March 11, 1898.[238,239] Both children were baptized at that address on June 20, 1898, by the Reverend S.G. Grove, minister at the Christian Street Methodist Episcopal Church.[240]

William Scott Chambers and his family moved to West Philadelphia in 1899.[241] They

---

[236]Conversation on August 12, 1995, with David Harrington Marshall, Jr., 262 S. Reese Street, Memphis, Tennessee 38111.

[237]Things That Aren't There Anymore - Temple University Edition, <<http://www.wrti.com/wrtifriend/things.html>>, downloaded August 4, 2016.

[238]The original Birth Certificate for Henry Graef (sic) Chambers, No. C52220, January 8, 1897, Philadelphia, Pennsylvania, was in the possession of the late William Scott Chambers, 325 N.W. 95th Avenue, Plantation, Florida 33324.

[239]The record of birth for Lucy Elizabeth Chambers could not be located in the following two microfilm records: 1898 Index to Births in Philadelphia, Philadelphia County, Pennsylvania, FHL Microfilm Rolls 1289357, 1289337.

[240]Pennsylvania and New Jersey, Church and Town Records, 1708-1985, Historical Society of Pennsylvania, Christian Street Methodist Episcopal Church, Record of Baptisms, Reel 342 says the baptisms of Henry Grafe Chambers and Lucy Elizabeth Chambers took place on June 20, 1898 at the residence, 1234 (sic) S. 34th Street.

[241]The Philadelphia city directories list the family at the following addresses:

1896	3223 Marston [later Lombard] Street; fireman, WP
1897	3223 Marston [later Lombard] Street, laborer, WP

were enumerated there in 1900 at the following location:

1329 ALDEN STREET, WEST PHILADELPHIA:

Chambers, William	Head W M b June 1867 PA 32 Married Engineer
-, Josie I.	Wife W F b July 1877 PA 22 Married
-. Harry G.	Son W M b Jan 1896 PA 3 Single
-, Lucy	Daughter W F b Mar 1898 PA 2 Single[242]

By 1909, the family had moved to a rented house where they were enumerated in 1910 as follows:

1842 S. CONESTOGA STREET, WEST PHILADELPHIA:

Chambers, William W. (sic)	Head M W 42 Married b PA Engineer Railroad
-, Josephine	Wife F W 32 Married b PA
-, Henry G.	Son M W 13 Single b PA
-, Lucy E.	Daughter F W 12 Single b PA[243]

From 1842 S. Conestoga Street, they moved to 5334 Greenway Avenue. Their daughter, Lucy Elizabeth (Chambers) Thompson, who was by then seriously ill with tuberculosis, and their baby granddaughter, Josephine, lived with them during this time period because their son-in-law, William Thompson, was away on active duty during World War I at a U.S. Army Air Corps base in Mount Clements, Michigan. Their son, Harry, was also away from home having enlisted in the U.S. Navy on April 30, 1917, and been called to active duty on October 2, 1917. Tragically, it was in their home at 5334 Greenway Avenue that their daughter died on November 22, 1918 of

---

1898	1232 S. 34th Street, engineer, South Philadelphia
1899	5504 Woodland Avenue, engineer, Kingsessing, WP
1900	1420 S. 55th Street, engineer, WP
1901	1347 S. 34th Street, engineer, South Philadelphia
1902-03	(inconclusive)
1904	1432 S. Conestoga Street, engineer, Kingsessing, WP
1905	1432 S. Conestoga Street, engineer, Kingsessing, WP
1906	4236 Woodland Avenue, engineer, Kingsessing, WP
1907-08	(inconclusive)
1909	1842 S. Conestoga Street, Kingsessing, WP

[242] 1900 U.S. Census (population), Pennsylvania, Philadelphia County, City of Philadelphia, Ward 40, E.D. 1017, page 7A, sheet 7, line 27, National Archives Microfilm Publication T623, Roll 1480.

[243] 1910 U.S. Census (population), Pennsylvania, Philadelphia County, City of Philadelphia, Ward 40, E.D. 1033, page 2A, line 32, Family Number 27, National Archives Microfilm Publication T624, Roll 1410.

tuberculosis.[244]

About a year after the death of their daughter, William Scott and Josephine (Reitze) Chambers bought a house about a block away at 5313 Yocum Street where the family was reunited after the end of World War I and enumerated in 1920 as follows:

5313 YOCUM STREET, WEST PHILADELPHIA:

Chambers, William S.	Head M W 53 Married b PA Engineer Railroad
-, Josephine	Wife F W 42 Married b PA
-, Henry H. (sic)	Son M W 21 Married b PA Fireman Railroad
-, Mary A.	DIL F W 23 Married b PA
Thompson, William	SIL M W 28 Widower b PA Salesman Automobile
-, Josephine H.	Grand-daughter F W 3-9/12 Single b PA [245]

William Scott and Josephine (Reitze) Chambers lived in the house at 5313 Yocum Street for the rest of their married lives.[246,247] It was there that they raised their only granddaughter and it was there that they celebrated their 50th Wedding Anniversary. Their grandson, William Scott Chambers, remembers that his grandparents' wedding anniversary celebration was held on the exact anniversary date of March 30, 1946, as far as he can recall. The anniversary was not a grand affair or a big party. They had dozens of friends all over West Philadelphia, but they did not invite a huge or even a small group to a big bash. It was not their style nor was it customary. What they did do was pass the word that it was their 50th Wedding Anniversary and they would be at home all day; that they were having an open house for all their neighbors, friends, fellow lodge members, and church members; and that refreshments would be served. Thus, William Scott Chambers and his wife, Josephine, celebrated their Golden Wedding Anniversary with people stopping by well into the night.[248]

---

[244]Death Certificate for Lucy Thompson, November 22, 1918, # 180521 & # 41448, Pennsylvania Department of Vital Statistics, New Castle, Pennsylvania.

[245]1920 U.S. Census (population), Pennsylvania, Philadelphia County, City of Philadelphia, Ward 40, E.D. 1499, page 4B, line 72, National Archives Microfilm Publication T625, Roll 1642.

[246]1930 U.S. Census (population), Pennsylvania, Philadelphia County, City of Philadelphia, Ward 40, E.D. 0214, page 16B, line 57, National Archives Microfilm Publication T626, Roll 2129.

[247]1940 U.S. Census (population), Pennsylvania, Philadelphia County, City of Philadelphia, Ward 51, E.D. 51-2238, page 3B, line 65, National Archives Microfilm Publication T627, Roll 3756.

[248]E-mail dated April 21, 2000, from the late William Scott Chambers, 325 N.W. 95th Avenue, Plantation, FL 33324-7021.

WORKING AS A FIREMAN. William Scott Chambers' first day at work as a fireman for the B&O Railroad was April 22, 1890.[249] An excellent description of what his work must have been like was published in *The Boston Globe*. It read as follows:

> It is doubtful that there is a man on the railroad train less appreciated than the fireman. When the fireman is at work, and that is nearly all the time when the wheels are turning, he stands, stooped over, shoveling in the fuel or raking in the coals in the fire box; his view ahead is obstructed; and he cannot see the danger that may be dashing upon him.
>
> The records show that more firemen than engineers are killed in railroad wrecks.
>
> About the only time a fireman has a little leisure is when a train is running down grade. Then "she is shut off", steam is saved and the knight of the shovel climbs up to a cushioned seat and takes a breathing spell. Even then one eye is ahead, his hand on the bell cord, and the other eye fastened on the steam gage. whose little black hands, fluctuating back and forth, gage his labor as well as the steam.
>
> There is a science in "feeding" an engine that is not understood by one not in the business. There is a way to throw in the coal and to empty the shovel and close the furnace door at the same time.
>
> It requires nice calculation that tells how many "scoop loads"are needed to keep the deck cabin clean, and a hundred other little things that go to make a skillful fireman - one that saves money for the company by husbanding the coal.
>
> In the old days the fireman on "wood burners"had a hard time of it and certainly earned the small money he received for his services, but he had a sinecure compared with the man in blue overalls and jumper who "stokes up"one of the huge "moguls" of the present day.
>
> These engines haul freight and eat up coal as if it were greased paper. The fireman is at work continuously, and about the only time he has to rest is when his train "takes a siding"to let a more aristocratic train pass.[250]

WORKING AS AN ENGINEER. Six years after starting work as the fireman, William Scott Chambers was promoted to the position of engineer for the B&O Railroad. Although he may have qualified for the position of engineer at an earlier date, those jobs were filled by seniority, and he would have had to wait until a position became available.

---

[249]Employment information for William Scott Chambers was in the possession of the late Josephine Thompson Marshall, 121 Reillywood Avenue, Haddonfield, New Jersey 08033.

[250]News Story, *The Boston Globe*, Saturday, February 26, 1922, p. 4.

As far as is known, William Scott Chambers worked at the B&O Railroad all his life.[251] In fact, as an engineer for the B&O Railroad, he is said to have logged a million miles at the throttle, but never left the City of Philadelphia because he spent all his time in the engine cab shifting locomotives within the city limits. He served in that capacity until he retired on January 31, 1938.[252, 253, 254] His picture along with an article that described his work appeared in the *Philadelphia Record*. It read as follows:

> "The farthest I ever got,"chuckled Engineer Bill Chambers as he retired from the Baltimore & Ohio Railroad yesterday after 47 years of service, "was shunting cars down to League Island."
>
> Now he's going to see something of the world.
>
> Chambers will soon be 71. He started to work for the railroad in 1890 as a fireman. Six years later he was promoted to an engineer, and served in that capacity ever since.
>
> He will draw a pension under the law which provides for retirement after 30 years' service of men past 60.
>
> But Bill doesn't feel old.
>
> "I'm just tired working," he smiled. "And my wife and I are going to have a little fun and see what's going on in the world."
>
> He brought his last engine to a halt in the freight yard at 36th and Jackson Streets at 2 PM. There was a small American flag fluttering on the big locomotive. Bill

---

[251]Conversation on April 27, 1996, with the late William Scott Chambers, 325 N.W. 95th Avenue, Plantation, FL 33324-7021.

[252]Employment records for William Scott Chambers were in the possession of the late Josephine Thompson Marshall, 121 Reillywood Avenue, Haddonfield, New Jersey 08033.

[253]The original Certificate of Annuity from the Railroad Retirement Board for William Scott Chambers dated April 18, 1938, was in the possession of the late William Scott Chambers, 325 N.W. 95th Avenue, Plantation, FL 33324-7021.

[254]Letter dated March 28, 1997, from Bill Poulos, Director of Public Affairs, Railroad Retirement Board, 844 North Rush Street, Chicago, IL 60611-2092 states that the claim folder for William Scott Chambers, SSN 705-09-5002, was destroyed in accordance with Federal records retention schedules. After the destruction of the claim folder, the only records in the possession of the Railroad Retirement Board are the service and earning statements from 1937 forward. A copy of these records was provided showing that William Scott Chambers was employed by the Baltimore and Ohio Railroad Company for twelve months in 1937 and earned $2,480.00. The report also shows that in 1938 and 1939 William Scott Chambers was employed by the Brotherhood of Locomotive Firemen and Enginemen in an administrative capacity.

put it there. Employees crowded around to shake hands with him. Later in the week they're going to give him a big party which officials will attend.

His son, Harry, was on hand to greet him. He's running his father a close second, with 22 years as a fireman on the Maryland division of the Pennsylvania Railroad.

The retiring Chambers lives at 5313 Yocum Street.[255,256]

BELONGING TO THE BROTHERHOOD. William Scott Chambers was a loyal member of the Brotherhood of Locomotive Firemen which was founded in 1873 at Port Jervis, New York, to provide mutual support for railroad firemen.[257] The teachings of its initiation ceremony were charity, industry, sobriety, and protection. Although the brotherhood initially emphasized insurance, it later branched out into labor-management relations.[258] In 1874, it established an Insurance Association to pay sick benefits at the option of local lodges, and death benefits by means of mutual assessments throughout the brotherhood. By 1899, the Brotherhood of Locomotive Firemen numbered more than 23,000 locomotive firemen on Canadian, Mexican, and American railways and had paid nearly $4 million in life and disability benefits over the preceding eighteen years.

Having made a commitment to working on the railroad, William Scott Chambers joined the Brotherhood of Locomotive Firemen on June 14, 1891.[259] Later, he is said to have founded and served as chairman of local Lodge # 319 of the Brotherhood of Locomotive Firemen and Enginemen, as the organization was known after 1906.[260] The headquarters of local Lodge # 319 was in a three story building at the corner of 63rd and Woodland Avenue where the members rented rooms above a bar on the first floor.

---

[255] New Story and Photograph, *Philadelphia Record*, Tuesday, February 1, 1938, p. 2.

[256] Photograph, *Philadelphia Inquirer*, Tuesday, February 1, 1938, p. 9.

[257] Albert C. Stevens, *The Cyclopedia of Fraternities - A Compilation of Existing Authentic Information and the Results of Original Investigations as to the Origin, Derivation, Founders, Development, Aims, Emblems, Character, and Personnel of More Than Six Hundred Secret Societies in the United States,* (New York: Hamilton Printing and Publishing Company, 1899), p. 383.

[258] National Union Catalog of Manuscript Collections, NUCMC, <<www.loc.gov/coll/nucmc/>>, downloaded April 22, 2000.

[259] Employment information for William Scott Chambers was in the possession of the late Josephine Thompson Marshall, 121 Reillywood Avenue, Haddonfield, New Jersey 08033.

[260] Conversation on November 25, 1999, with the late Josephine Thompson Marshall, 121 Reillywood Avenue, Haddonfield, New Jersey 08033.

There was also a ladies' auxiliary of the brotherhood to which William Scott Chambers' wife, Josephine, belonged.[261] The ladies' society of the Brotherhood of Locomotive Firemen and Enginemen was recognized as an auxiliary of the brotherhood at its second biennial convention in 1890. The ladies' auxiliary was organized for the purpose of rendering assistance, encouraging the brotherhood in its good work, extending a hand of charity, helping each other in time of need, and elevating their social and intellectual standing. It was also the aim of the ladies' auxiliary to cultivate a spirit of harmony, to promote sociability, and to draw into friendly and affectionate relationship the lady members of the families of the brotherhood.[262]

Even though William Scott Chambers only went as far as the fourth grade in school, he was a good writer and singlehandedly composed all his union speeches.[263] He was influential at both the local and the national levels of the organization and even sponsored a member of the brotherhood for a leadership position in the national organization. William Scott Chambers was instrumental in holding the local lodge together during a wildcat strike and he attended at least one convention of the national organization in San Antonio, Texas.

On the occasion of his retirement, he was given a gold pin by the members of his local lodge which he always wore on his lapel with pride as it commemorated his many years of loyal service to the brotherhood.[264]

DEATH OF WILLIAM SCOTT CHAMBERS. William Scott Chambers died on February 5, 1950, at the age of 83 from cerebral thrombosis.[265] His obituary appeared in the *Philadelphia Inquirer* as follows:

> CHAMBERS - Of 5313 Yocum st., Feb 5, WILLIAM S., husband of Josephine
> I. Relatives and friends also Lodge 319 B. of L. E. and F. are invited to services
> Wed. at 2 P.M., from Barker's 5413 Chester ave. Int. private. Viewing Tues. 7 to
> 9 P.M.[266]

---

[261]Obituary of Josephine I. Chambers, *Philadelphia Inquirer*, Saturday, May 5, 1962, p. 7.

[262]National Union Catalog of Manuscript Collections, NUCMC, <<www.loc.gov/coll/nucmc/>>, downloaded April 22, 2000.

[263]Conversation on April 18, 1997, with the late William Scott Chambers, 325 N.W. 95th Avenue, Plantation, FL 33324-7021.

[264]Conversation on November 25, 1999, with the late Josephine Thompson Marshall, 121 Reillywood Avenue, Haddonfield, New Jersey 08033.

[265]Death Certificate for William Scott Chambers, February 5, 1950, # 15795 & # 2559, Pennsylvania Division of Vital Statistics, New Castle, Pennsylvania.

[266]Obituary, *Philadelphia Inquirer*, Monday, February 6, 1950, p. 24.

His funeral was well attended by family, friends, neighbors, fellow lodge members, and members of his church. A true and loyal member of the Brotherhood of Locomotive Firemen and Enginemen, he was buried with his gold pin securely fastened to his lapel.

DEATH OF JOSEPHINE (REITZE) CHAMBERS. Soon after the death of William Scott Chambers, his widow, Josephine, moved to the Evangelical Home at 8401 Roosevelt Boulevard. It was there that she died on May 3, 1962, of chronic myocarditis and arteriosclerotic cardio vascular disease.[267] Her obituary appeared in the *Philadelphia Inquirer* as follows:

> CHAMBERS - May 3, 1962, JOSEPHINE I., (nee Reitze) of the Evangelical Home, widow of William S. Chambers (aged 84 years). Relatives, friends and members of Pride of William Penn Lodge # 433, B. L. F. E., are invited to services, Mon., 1 P.M. at Hackman Bros., Inc., 905-07 W. Lehigh ave., where friends may call Sun. eve. Int. Mt. Moriah Cemetery.[268]

MOUNT MORIAH CEMETERY, PHILADELPHIA, PENNSYLVANIA. William Scott Chambers and Josephine (Reitze) Chambers are buried in Mount Moriah Cemetery which is located at 62nd and Kingsessing Avenue in West Philadelphia.[269]

There is a fairly large headstone engraved with a Masonic insignia on the plot.[270] The headstone reads simply:

CHAMBERS
THOMPSON

There are no footstones on the plot.

Also buried in the same plot with William Scott Chambers and his wife, Josephine (Reitze) Chambers, are their two children and their spouses.

That is, their daughter, Lucy Elizabeth (Chambers) Thompson, and her spouse, William

---

[267]Death Certificate for Josephine Irene Chambers, May 3, 1962, # not shown, Pennsylvania Division of Vital Statistics, New Castle, Pennsylvania.

[268]Obituary, *Philadelphia Inquirer*, Saturday, May 5, 1962, p. 7.

[269]The original deed for the plot at Mount Moriah Cemetery (10 Middle Part of South Part, Range 7, Section E, aka Section E, Range 7, Lot 10) was in the possession of the late William Scott Chambers, 325 N.W. 95th Avenue, Plantation, Florida 33324.

[270]William Scott Chambers' son, Henry Grafe Chambers, and his son-in-law, William Thompson, both of whom are buried in this plot, were members of the Masons.

Thompson.[271,272] And, their son, Henry Grafe Chambers, and his spouse, Mary Ann (McCauley) Chambers.[273,274,275,276]

Together, forever.

---

[271]Obituary, *Philadelphia Inquirer*, Monday, November 25, 1918, p. 15 and Tuesday, November 26, 1918, p. 15.

> THOMPSON - Nov 22, LUCY ELIZABETH, wife of William Thompson and daughter of W.S. and Josephine Chambers, aged 20. Relatives and friends are invited to services, Tues., 2 p.m., 5334 Greenway ave. Int. Mt. Moriah Cem. Friends may call Mon., 7:30 to 9:30 p.m.

[272]Obituary, *The Evening Bulletin*, Monday, June 21, 1965, p. 14.

> THOMPSON - Of 121 Reillywood ave., Haddonfield, N.J., on June 19, 1965, WILLIAM, husband of the late Lucy Chambers Thompson. Services for relatives and friends on Wed., at 1 PM at Oliver H. Bair's 1820 Chestnut st., where friends may call Tues., 7 to 9 PM. Int. Mt. Moriah Cem.

[273]Death Certificate for Henry G. Chambers, November 11, 1953, # not shown, State of New Jersey, Office of Registrar of Vital Statistics of Borough of Collingswood, Camden County.

[274]Obituary, *Philadelphia Inquirer*, Thursday, November 12, 1953, p. 41 and Friday, November 13, 1953, p 40.

> CHAMBERS - On Nov. 11, 1953, HARRY G., husband of Mary McCauley Chambers, aged 56 years. Relatives and friends, also B of LE No. 51 are invited to attend the funeral services Mon., 11 A.M., at the Murray Funeral Home, 408 Cooper Street, Camden, N.J. Viewing Sunday evening.

[275]Death Certificate for Maryann (sic) Chambers, August 8, 1984, # 84-537, State of New Jersey, Office of Registrar of Vital Statistics of Burlington Township, Burlington County.

[276]Obituary, *Philadelphia Inquirer*, Saturday, August 11, 1984, p. 10-A.

> CHAMBERS - On August 8, 1984, MARYANN wife of the late Henry G. Chambers and mother of the late Thomas W. Chambers at the Masonic Home, Burlington, N.J. She is survived by her son William S. Chambers, 3 granddaughters, Kathryn Torpey, Cynthia S. Chambers and Joann Smith. Funeral services were held Fri. 10:30 AM at the Masonic Home Chapel, Burlington, N.J. Int. was in Mt. Moriah Cem., Phila.

Descendants of George Chambers

Generation 1

1. **GEORGE[1] CHAMBERS** was born about 1815 in Ireland. He died on 03 May 1868 in Philadelphia Pennsylvania. He married Elizabeth in Ireland. She was born about 1818 in Ireland. She died on 06 Oct 1862 in Philadelphia, Pennsylvania.

George Chambers and Elizabeth had the following children:

2. i. GEORGE WASHINGTON[2] CHAMBERS was born on 22 Feb 1841 in Philadelphia, Pennsylvania. He died on 09 May 1906 in Philadelphia, Pennsylvania. He married Annie Adam Edwards, daughter of Adam Edwards and Isabella Scott on 04 Jul 1866 in Philadelphia, Pennsylvania. She was born on 26 Feb 1847 in Edinburgh, Midlothian, Scotland. She died on 27 Dec 1927 in Philadelphia, Pennsylvania.

    ii. WILLIAM CHAMBERS was born in 1842 in Philadelphia Pennsylvania. He died on 31 Aug 1866 in Philadelphia Pennsylvania.

3. iii. EMMA CHAMBERS was born in 1844 in Philadelphia, Pennsylvania. She died on 26 Dec 1883 in Philadelphia, Pennsylvania. She married John Clark, son of Thomas C. Clark and Ann about 1864. He was born about 1840 in Ireland.

Generation 2

2. **GEORGE WASHINGTON[2] CHAMBERS** (George[1]) was born on 22 Feb 1841 in Philadelphia, Pennsylvania. He died on 09 May 1906 in Philadelphia, Pennsylvania. He married Annie Adam Edwards, daughter of Adam Edwards and Isabella Scott on 04 Jul 1866 in Philadelphia, Pennsylvania. She was born on 26 Feb 1847 in Edinburgh, Midlothian, Scotland. She died on 27 Dec 1927 in Philadelphia, Pennsylvania.

George Washington Chambers and Annie Adam Edwards had the following children:

4. i. WILLIAM SCOTT[3] CHAMBERS was born on 05 Jun 1867 in Philadelphia, Pennsylvania. He died on 05 Feb 1950 in Philadelphia, Pennsylvania. He married (1) SARAH WHITE, daughter of Richard White and Catharine on 01 Feb 1894 in Philadelphia, Pennsylvania. She was born on 15 Oct 1868 in Philadelphia, Pennsylvania. She died on 14 Aug 1894 in Philadelphia, Pennsylvania. He married (2) JOSEPHINE IRENE REITZE, daughter of Christopher Reitze and Lucy S. Devlin on 30 Mar 1896 in Philadelphia, Pennsylvania. She was born on 04 Jul 1877 in Philadelphia, Pennsylvania. She died on 03 May 1962 in Philadelphia, Pennsylvania.

    ii. ELIZA JANE CHAMBERS was born on 23 Oct 1869 in Philadelphia, Pennsylvania. She died on 18 Nov 1871 in Philadelphia, Pennsylvania.

5. iii. LYDIA E. CHAMBERS was born on 27 Feb 1872 in Philadelphia, Pennsylvania. She died on 19 Feb 1949 in Philadelphia, Pennsylvania. She married (1) LEONARD H. SCHMIDT, son of Ernest Schmidt and Caroline on 25 Aug 1909 in Philadelphia, Pennsylvania. He was born on 13 Jul 1878 in Germany. He died on 14 Feb 1915 in Philadelphia Pennsylvania. She married (2) JOHN J. ROE, son of Frank Roe and Delia Murphy on 12 Sep 1916 in Philadelphia, Philadelphia County, Pennsylvania. He was born on 01 May 1870 in New York. He died on 15 Oct 1929 in Philadelphia, Pennsylvania.

6. iv. EMMA CLARK CHAMBERS was born on 23 Mar 1875 in Philadelphia, Pennsylvania. She died on 04 Oct 1960 in Newtown Square, Delaware County, Pennsylvania. She married William Young Spence, son of George Spence and Mary Young on 20 Mar 1899 in Delaware County Pennsylvania. He was born on 09 Feb 1870 in Scotland.

He died on 31 Dec 1943 in Philadelphia, Pennsylvania.

     v.   ANNIE I. CHAMBERS was born on 12 Feb 1878 in Philadelphia, Pennsylvania. She died on 06 Jan 1944 in Philadelphia, Pennsylvania.

7.   vi.   GEORGE EDWARDS CHAMBERS was born on 01 Jul 1880 in Philadelphia, Pennsylvania. He died on 26 Jun 1937 in Philadelphia, Pennsylvania. He married Annie Richards, daughter of David P. Richards and Susanna Thomas on 24 Apr 1905 in Philadelphia, Pennsylvania. She was born on 05 Jun 1880 in Philadelphia, Pennsylvania. She died on 17 Jan 1953 in Philadelphia, Pennsylvania.

     vii.   ELIZABETH H. CHAMBERS was born on 01 Sep 1883 in Philadelphia, Pennsylvania. She died on 18 Jan 1911 in Philadelphia, Pennsylvania. She married Joseph W. McManus on 16 Apr 1907 in Philadelphia, Pennsylvania. He was born on 17 Sep 1882 in Ireland. He died on 08 Oct 1918 in Philadelphiia, Pennsylvania.

3.   **EMMA**[2] **CHAMBERS** (George[1]) was born in 1844 in Philadelphia, Pennsylvania. She died on 26 Dec 1883 in Philadelphia, Pennsylvania. She married John Clark, son of Thomas C. Clark and Ann about 1864. He was born about 1840 in Ireland.

John Clark and Emma Chambers had the following children:

     i.   THOMAS[3] CLARK was born on 27 Oct 1865 in Philadelphia, Pennsylvania. He died about 09 Nov 1865 in Philadelphia, Pennsylvania.

8.   ii.   THOMAS JOHN CLARK was born on 03 Jan 1867 in Philadelphia, Pennsylvania. He died on 25 Jan 1949 in Philadelphia, Pennsylvania. He married Annie McIntyre, daughter of Donald McIntyre and Mary on 27 Apr 1898 in Philadelphia, Philadelphia County, Pennsylvania. She was born on 25 Dec 1867 in Ireland. She died on 31 Dec 1947 in Philadelphia, Pennsylvania.

9.   iii.   EMMA ROSE CLARK was born on 28 Feb 1871 in Philadelphia, Pennsylvania. She died on 07 Sep 1949 in Philadelphia, Pennsylvania. She married Albert Frederick Winkel, son of Albert Winkel and Mary Ann Schneck in 1905 in Philadelphia, Pennsylvania. He was born on 26 Nov 1873 in Philadelphia, Pennsylvania. He died after 1949.

Generation 3

4.   **WILLIAM SCOTT**[3] **CHAMBERS** (George Washington[2], George[1]) was born on 05 Jun 1867 in Philadelphia, Pennsylvania. He died on 05 Feb 1950 in Philadelphia, Pennsylvania. He married (1) **SARAH WHITE**, daughter of Richard White and Catharine on 01 Feb 1894 in Philadelphia, Pennsylvania. She was born on 15 Oct 1868 in Philadelphia, Pennsylvania. She died on 14 Aug 1894 in Philadelphia, Pennsylvania. He married (2) **JOSEPHINE IRENE REITZE**, daughter of Christopher Reitze and Lucy S. Devlin on 30 Mar 1896 in Philadelphia, Pennsylvania. She was born on 04 Jul 1877 in Philadelphia, Pennsylvania. She died on 03 May 1962 in Philadelphia, Pennsylvania.

William Scott Chambers and Josephine Irene Reitze had the following children:

10.   i.   HENRY GRAFE[4] CHAMBERS was born on 08 Jan 1897 in Philadelphia, Pennsylvania. He died on 11 Nov 1953 in Collingswood, Camden County, New Jersey. He married Mary Ann McCauley, daughter of Thomas McCauley and Mary Ann Wallace on 30 Jul 1918 in Philadelphia, Pennsylvania. She was born on 07 Jul 1892 in Philadelphia, Pennsylvania. She died on 08 Aug 1984 in Burlington Township,

Burlington County, New Jersey.

11.   ii.   LUCY ELIZABETH CHAMBERS was born on 11 Mar 1898 in Philadelphia, Pennsylvania. She died on 22 Nov 1918 in Philadelphia, Pennsylvania. She married William Thompson, son of William Thompson and Hester Carrick on 12 Jun 1915 in Elkton, Cecil County, Maryland. He was born on 28 May 1891 in Pennsylvania. He died on 19 Jun 1965 in Philadelphia, Pennsylvania.

5.   LYDIA E.³ CHAMBERS (George Washington², George¹) was born on 27 Feb 1872 in Philadelphia, Pennsylvania. She died on 19 Feb 1949 in Philadelphia, Pennsylvania. She married (1) LEONARD H. SCHMIDT, son of Ernest Schmidt and Caroline on 25 Aug 1909 in Philadelphia, Pennsylvania. He was born on 13 Jul 1878 in Germany. He died on 14 Feb 1915 in Philadelphia Pennsylvania. She married (2) JOHN J. ROE, son of Frank Roe and Delia Murphy on 12 Sep 1916 in Philadelphia, Philadelphia County, Pennsylvania. He was born on 01 May 1870 in New York. He died on 15 Oct 1929 in Philadelphia, Pennsylvania.

Leonard H. Schmidt and Lydia E. Chambers had the following child:

12.   i.   MARTHA⁴ SCHMIDT was born on 16 Oct 1910 in Pennsylvania. She died on 05 Aug 1990 in Pennsylvania. She married JOSEPH WILLIAM HASSELL. He was born on 15 Jan 1913 in Philadelphia Pennsylvania. He died on 27 Apr 1940 in Philadelphia Pennsylvania.

6.   EMMA CLARK³ CHAMBERS (George Washington², George¹) was born on 23 Mar 1875 in Philadelphia, Pennsylvania. She died on 04 Oct 1960 in Newtown Square, Delaware County, Pennsylvania. She married William Young Spence, son of George Spence and Mary Young on 20 Mar 1899 in Delaware County Pennsylvania. He was born on 09 Feb 1870 in Scotland. He died on 31 Dec 1943 in Philadelphia, Pennsylvania.

William Young Spence and Emma Clark Chambers had the following children:

13.   i.   PAULINE L.⁴ SPENCE was born on 22 Jul 1899 in Philadelphia, Pennsylvania. She died on 17 Dec 1959 in Philadelphia, Pennsylvania. She married WILLIAM FREDERICK GURK SR.. He was born on 21 Sep 1897 in Philadelphia, Pennsylvania. He died on 20 Jan 1981 in Hartford, Hartford County, Connecticut.

    ii.   LYDIA VIOLA SPENCE was born on 09 Jun 1902 in Pennsylvania. She died on 21 Aug 1989 in Lee County Florida. She married George Clemens Enge, son of Laura Louise in 1928 in Philadelphia, Pennsylvania. He was born on 17 Aug 1900 in Pennsylvania. He died on 26 Dec 1987 in Collier County Florida.

14.   iii.   WILLIAM YOUNG SPENCE JR. was born on 12 Nov 1904 in Philadelphia, Pennsylvania. He died on 29 Jan 1954 in Philadelphia Pennsylvania. He married Mae A. Prescott, daughter of father Prescott and Freda A on 05 Aug 1938 in Delaware County Pennsylvania. She was born in 1913 in Pennsylvania.

    iv.   GEORGE E. SPENCE was born on 09 Jun 1908 in Pennsylvania. He died on 14 May 1983 in Stone Harbor, Cape May County, New Jersey. He married Marie E. Priggemeier on 17 Jun 1938 in Philadelphia, Pennsylvania. She was born on 24 May 1909 in Pennsylvania. She died on 19 Sep 2002 in Stone Harbor, Cape May County, New Jersey.

7.   GEORGE EDWARDS³ CHAMBERS (George Washington², George¹) was born on 01 Jul 1880 in Philadelphia, Pennsylvania. He died on 26 Jun 1937 in Philadelphia, Pennsylvania. He married

Annie Richards, daughter of David P. Richards and Susanna Thomas on 24 Apr 1905 in Philadelphia, Pennsylvania. She was born on 05 Jun 1880 in Philadelphia, Pennsylvania. She died on 17 Jan 1953 in Philadelphia, Pennsylvania.

George Edwards Chambers and Annie Richards had the following children:

- i. ANNIE[4] CHAMBERS was born on 24 Jun 1907 in Philadelphia, Pennsylvania. She died on 24 Jun 1907 in Philadelphia, Pennsylvania.

15. ii. GEORGE RICHARDS CHAMBERS SR. was born on 14 Sep 1908 in Philadelphia, Pennsylvania. He died on 29 Sep 1984 in Philadelphia, Pennsylvania. He married Mary Luciano in 1934 in Philadelphia, Philadelphia County, Pennsylvania. She was born on 24 Aug 1913 in Philadelphia, Pennsylvania. She died on 24 Jan 1979 in Philadelphia, Pennsylvania.

- iii. GERTRUDE HELEN CHAMBERS was born in Dec 1910 in Washington, D.C.. She died on 18 Mar 1911 in Washington, D.C..

8. **THOMAS JOHN[3] CLARK** (Emma[2] Chambers, George[1] Chambers) was born on 03 Jan 1867 in Philadelphia, Pennsylvania. He died on 25 Jan 1949 in Philadelphia, Pennsylvania. He married Annie McIntyre, daughter of Donald McIntyre and Mary on 27 Apr 1898 in Philadelphia, Philadelphia County, Pennsylvania. She was born on 25 Dec 1867 in Ireland. She died on 31 Dec 1947 in Philadelphia, Pennsylvania.

Thomas John Clark and Annie McIntyre had the following children:

- i. THOMAS[4] CLARK was born about Oct 1896 in Philadelphia, Philadelphia County, Pennsylvania. He died on 22 Dec 1896 in Philadelphia, Philadelphia County, Pennsylvania.

16. ii. FRANCIS "FRANK" CLARK was born on 19 Oct 1898 in Philadelphia, Pennsylvania. He died in Sep 1982 in Philadelphia, Pennsylvania. He married Kathryn L. Geary, daughter of Joseph Geary and Bridget Bryer in 1931 in Philadelphia, Philadelphia County, Pennsylvania. She was born on 26 Apr 1906 in Philadelphia, Pennsylvania. She died on 24 Dec 1941 in Philadelphia, Pennsylvania.

- iii. RAYMOND CLARK was born in May 1903 in Philadelphia, Pennsylvania. He died on 08 Mar 1917 in Philadelphia, Philadelphia County, Pennsylvania.

9. **EMMA ROSE[3] CLARK** (Emma[2] Chambers, George[1] Chambers) was born on 28 Feb 1871 in Philadelphia, Pennsylvania. She died on 07 Sep 1949 in Philadelphia, Pennsylvania. She married Albert Frederick Winkel, son of Albert Winkel and Mary Ann Schneck in 1905 in Philadelphia, Pennsylvania. He was born on 26 Nov 1873 in Philadelphia, Pennsylvania. He died after 1949.

Albert Frederick Winkel and Emma Rose Clark had the following children:

- i. MARY ANN[4] WINKEL was born on 14 Jun 1906 in Philadelphia, Pennsylvania. She died on 15 Jun 1906 in Philadelphia, Pennsylvania.

- ii. MARY E. WINKEL was born in 1908 in Philadelphia, Pennsylvania. She died after 1963.

- iii. JOHN "TWIN" WINKEL was born on 06 Oct 1911 in Philadelphia, Pennsylvania. He died on 06 Oct 1911 in Philadelphia, Pennsylvania.

Appendix A

iv. ALBERT F. "TWIN" WINKEL JR. was born on 06 Oct 1911 in Philadelphia, Pennsylvania. He died on 06 Apr 1980 in Fort Lauderdale, Broward County, Florida. He married MARY MENDHAM. She was born on 20 May 1918 in Dayton, Greene, Ohio. She died on 21 Aug 2012 in Hot Springs, Arkansas.

Generation 4

10. **HENRY GRAFE[4] CHAMBERS** (William Scott[3], George Washington[2], George[1]) was born on 08 Jan 1897 in Philadelphia, Pennsylvania. He died on 11 Nov 1953 in Collingswood, Camden County, New Jersey. He married Mary Ann McCauley, daughter of Thomas McCauley and Mary Ann Wallace on 30 Jul 1918 in Philadelphia, Pennsylvania. She was born on 07 Jul 1892 in Philadelphia, Pennsylvania. She died on 08 Aug 1984 in Burlington Township, Burlington County, New Jersey.

Henry Grafe Chambers and Mary Ann McCauley had the following children:

    i. WILLIAM SCOTT[5] CHAMBERS was born on 25 Feb 1921 in Philadelphia, Pennsylvania. He died on 08 Feb 2014 in Plantation Broward County Florida. He married Gloria Ann Freda, daughter of Guerino Angelo Maria Freda and Filomena M. Quaresima on 26 Jan 1946 in Princeton, Mercer County, New Jersey. She was born on 06 Mar 1921 in Princeton, Mercer County, New Jersey. She died on 28 Aug 1987 in Portsmouth, Virginia.

    ii. THOMAS WALLACE CHAMBERS was born on 25 Mar 1923 in Philadelphia, Pennsylvania. He died on 06 Oct 1955 in Stateburg, Sumter County, South Carolina. He married Florence Clark, daughter of James Freeman Clark and Anna Lee on 31 May 1948 in New Castle, New Castle County, Delaware. She was born on 13 Apr 1930 in Haddonfield, Camden County, New Jersey. She died on 16 Feb 2016 in Churchville, Bucks County, Pennsylvania.

11. **LUCY ELIZABETH[4] CHAMBERS** (William Scott[3], George Washington[2], George[1]) was born on 11 Mar 1898 in Philadelphia, Pennsylvania. She died on 22 Nov 1918 in Philadelphia, Pennsylvania. She married William Thompson, son of William Thompson and Hester Carrick on 12 Jun 1915 in Elkton, Cecil County, Maryland. He was born on 28 May 1891 in Pennsylvania. He died on 19 Jun 1965 in Philadelphia, Pennsylvania.

William Thompson and Lucy Elizabeth Chambers had the following child:

    i. JOSEPHINE HESTER[5] THOMPSON was born on 10 May 1916 in Philadelphia, Pennsylvania. She died on 06 Oct 2008 in Haddonfield, Camden County, New Jersey. She married David Harrington Marshall Sr., son of Thomas Marshall on 13 Jun 1942 in Philadelphia, Pennsylvania. He was born on 27 Jun 1912 in Philadelphia, Pennsylvania. He died on 02 Nov 2009 in Newark, Delaware.

12. **MARTHA[4] SCHMIDT** (Lydia E.[3] Chambers, George Washington[2] Chambers, George[1] Chambers) was born on 16 Oct 1910 in Pennsylvania. She died on 05 Aug 1990 in Pennsylvania. She married **JOSEPH WILLIAM HASSELL**. He was born on 15 Jan 1913 in Philadelphia Pennsylvania. He died on 27 Apr 1940 in Philadelphia Pennsylvania.

Joseph William Hassell and Martha Schmidt had the following child:

    i. JOSEPH WILLIAM[5] HASSELL JR. was born on 22 Jun 1935 in Philadelphia, Pennsylvania. He died on 29 Sep 2006 in Philadelphia, Pennsylvania. He married FRANCES MARIE BARBER. She was born on 05 Oct 1941 in Philadelphia Pennsylvania. She died on 28 Aug 2007.

13. **PAULINE L.**[4] **SPENCE** (Emma Clark[3] Chambers, George Washington[2] Chambers, George[1] Chambers) was born on 22 Jul 1899 in Philadelphia, Pennsylvania. She died on 17 Dec 1959 in Philadelphia, Pennsylvania. She married **WILLIAM FREDERICK GURK SR.**. He was born on 21 Sep 1897 in Philadelphia, Pennsylvania. He died on 20 Jan 1981 in Hartford, Hartford County, Connecticut.

William Frederick Gurk Sr. and Pauline L. Spence had the following child:

    i.   WILLIAM FREDERICK[5] GURK JR. was born on 04 Feb 1919 in Philadelphia, Pennsylvania. He died on 27 Sep 2010 in Philadelphia, Pennsylvania. He married Gertrude E. Murtagh in 1945 in Philadelphia, Pennsylvania. She was born about 1924 in Pennsylvania. She died after 2008.

14. **WILLIAM YOUNG**[4] **SPENCE JR.** (Emma Clark[3] Chambers, George Washington[2] Chambers, George[1] Chambers) was born on 12 Nov 1904 in Philadelphia, Pennsylvania. He died on 29 Jan 1954 in Philadelphia Pennsylvania. He married Mae A. Prescott, daughter of father Prescott and Freda A on 05 Aug 1938 in Delaware County Pennsylvania. She was born in 1913 in Pennsylvania.

William Young Spence Jr. and Mae A. Prescott had the following child:

    i.   WILLIAM "BILLY"[5] SPENCE was born about 1941.

15. **GEORGE RICHARDS**[4] **CHAMBERS SR.** (George Edwards[3], George Washington[2], George[1]) was born on 14 Sep 1908 in Philadelphia, Pennsylvania. He died on 29 Sep 1984 in Philadelphia, Pennsylvania. He married Mary Luciano in 1934 in Philadelphia, Philadelphia County, Pennsylvania. She was born on 24 Aug 1913 in Philadelphia, Pennsylvania. She died on 24 Jan 1979 in Philadelphia, Pennsylvania.

George Richards Chambers Sr. and Mary Luciano had the following children:

    i.   GEORGE RICHARDS[5] CHAMBERS JR. was born on 25 Jul 1934 in Philadelphia, Pennsylvania. He married (1) RUTH KEPHARDT about 1958. He married (2) LOIS K. LAFFERTY, daughter of Harry Lafferty and Lydia Helen Butterfield on 06 Nov 1977. She was born on 06 Mar 1933. She died on 21 Feb 2003 in Pennsylvania.

    ii.   DOROTHY ANNA CHAMBERS was born on 12 Jan 1936 in Philadelphia, Pennsylvania. She died on 17 Jul 2012 in Newark, New Castle County, Delaware. She married Alton Lamar Brooks on 03 Mar 1956. He was born on 03 Sep 1930. He died on 31 Jan 1993 in Delaware.

    iii.   JOSEPH D. CHAMBERS SR. was born on 30 Dec 1936 in Philadelphia, Pennsylvania. He died on 03 May 2013 in Wilmington, Delaware. He married Joan F. Walker on 24 Jan 1964 in Collingdale, Delaware County Pennsylvania. She was born on 04 Apr 1932 in Pennsylvania.

16. **FRANCIS "FRANK"**[4] **CLARK** (Thomas John[3], Emma[2] Chambers, George[1] Chambers) was born on 19 Oct 1898 in Philadelphia, Pennsylvania. He died in Sep 1982 in Philadelphia, Pennsylvania. He married Kathryn L. Geary, daughter of Joseph Geary and Bridget Bryer in 1931 in Philadelphia, Philadelphia County, Pennsylvania. She was born on 26 Apr 1906 in Philadelphia, Pennsylvania. She died on 24 Dec 1941 in Philadelphia, Pennsylvania.

Francis "Frank" Clark and Kathryn L. Geary had the following child:

    i.   ANN F.[5] CLARK was born in 1932 in Philadelphia, Pennsylvania. She died on 17 Jul 1987 in Philadelphia, Pennsylvania. She married SAMUEL SCHWARTZ. He was born on 28 Jul 1916. He died on 04 Jul 1989 in Philadelphia, Pennsylvania.

My Chambers Family, An Oral History
by William Scott Chambers[*]
July 2000

MY BIRTH

My name is William Scott Chambers. I was named after my paternal grandfather. I was born February 25, 1921, at the Presbyterian Hospital in Philadelphia. At the time, I think we were living at 1631 S. 53rd Street. My mother told me that it was a difficult birth and that she and I almost died. I was badly banged up by the use of forceps that crushed part of my scull resulting in partial paralysis on my right side.

MY FAMILY

My mother's full name was Mary Ann McCauley. She was born on July 7, 1892, in Philadelphia. She was baptized at Tabor Presbyterian Church.[1] My father's full name was Henry Grafe Chambers. He was named after his uncle, Henry Grafe Douglass. My father was born January 8, 1897, in Philadelphia on Gray's Ferry Road. He was baptized in the Methodist Church, but I never knew the name of the church.

I only had one brother, Thomas Wallace Chambers. He was named after our maternal grandfather. He was born March 25, 1923, at home, with no apparent complications, while we were living at 1547 S. Lindenwood Street. My brother and I got along well as I only remember one fight with my brother and I don't remember why. My brother was in the U.S. Army Air Corps in World War II. He survived a mid-air collision during the war via an emergency parachute jump on July 8, 1944 over Rutland County, England.[2] He fell 700 feet, pulled the cord at 200 feet, and the parachute opened at 45 feet. The vicar of the village where my brother was found after the parachute drop wrote a letter to my mother describing the entire event which he witnessed from the ground. It was a beautiful letter. I don't know whatever became of it.

My brother got out of the U.S. Army Air Corps in 1946 after having served in World War II. He went to work for the Pennsylvania Reading Seashore Line as a passenger brakeman (i.e., brakeman/ticket taker). Then, he went to college at Glassboro State for two years. In 1948, he joined the Air Force as a Cadet to became a pilot. I remember that he was accepted as an Air Force Cadet in 1948. He was to go to Randolph, Texas by train for training as a pilot. My parents and I along with your Aunt Florence took my brother to the Philadelphia train station in July 1948. In 1948, you could not be married and be an Air Force Cadet. After the train left the station, your Aunt Florence told my parents that she and my brother were secretly married.

---

[*]As told to his daughter, Kathryn C. Torpey. © 2000 by Kathryn C. Torpey, 5035 Domain Place, Alexandria, Virginia 22311-5066. All rights reserved.

As a child, I was called Bill or Billy. My father was called Harry and my brother was called Tom. No other nicknames. My father was a fireman and an engineer on the Pennsylvania Railroad which he joined in 1916. He was promoted to Road Foreman of Engines on the Pennsylvania Reading Seashore Line in 1942. My mother did not work outside the home after she was married.

My parents were married by a Methodist Episcopal minister at the minister's house at 51st and Greenway Avenue in Philadelphia[3]. My father had come down from New York where his U.S. Navy ship had come in to port during World War I. Pauline and Fred Queroli went with them as witnesses while my grandfather, Thomas McCauley, stayed home to cook the supper.[4]

My father was in the U.S. Navy from April 1917 to April 29, 1921.[5,6] He made three trips across the Atlantic and to San Diego, California, on the U.S.S. Peter H. Crowell, a cargo and ammo ship. The United States entered World War I on April 2, 1917, and my father enlisted for four years in the Naval Reserve on April 30, 1917 in Philadelphia with his mother listed as dependent relative followed by his father. The record shows they all lived at 5334 Greenwood Avenue, but that is a mistake. I know they lived on Greenway Avenue in the 5300 block just west of 53rd Street next door to the Thompson family whom I knew very well.

My father enlisted on April 30, but apparently was called to active service on October 2, 1917 and assigned to Wissahicken Naval Station for basic training. He was assigned to the U.S.S. Peter H. Crowell from January 1, 1918 to March 27, 1919. He was then transferred to a receiving station and the U.S.S. Manna Hatta until April 24, 1919 when he was released from active service. His four year enlistment was up and he was honorably discharged on April 29, 1921. Obviously, he was not drafted. His address on expiration of his enrollment is listed on his certificate dated April 29, 1921 as Yocum Street. This is incorrect as I was born while my parents were living at 1631 S. 53rd Street in February 1921.

My father was a member of the Masonic Lodge in Camden, New Jersey, not Philadelphia.[7] He was a member of the Masonic Lodge and the various levels therein such as Blue Lodge and Chapter, etc. He was also a member of the Shriners in Camden. Now that I've said that, I don't remember the name or number of the local lodge at this time. I found my father's Masonic Apron and also a green pointed hat from the Shrine Temple to which he belonged with two inscriptions one of which says Tall Cedars of Lebanon and the other which reads Camden Forest No. 5. Somewhere there is probably a Masonic ID card, but I don't know where. My father joined the Masons when they were living on Baird Boulevard in Camden where they moved in the spring of 1942 as far as I can recall. My mother joined the Eastern Star about that time.[8] When I returned from my World War II Russian disaster at the end of July 1942, my parents were living in New Jersey.

My father never went past the eighth grade in Benjamin B. Comegy grammar school. His first job was as a delivery boy for Sukins Market. It was after that job that he became a call boy on the B&O Railroad at 58th and Woodland Avenue. He became a fireman on steam locomotives on the Maryland Division of the Pennsylvania Railroad in May 1916 and was later promoted to the position of locomotive engineer. In early 1942, he was transferred to the Pennsylvania Reading Seashore Line as Road Foreman of Engines where he worked until he died[9,10]

As I said, my father began work in 1916. In 1936, he was working the New York, Philadelphia, Washington route. Whenever he would take a train as far south as Washington, he would spend the night in Alexandria, Virginia, at a freight yard called Potomac Yard. At times, he was on the pilot train that was sent ahead of the train with the President on board. My father was qualified as an engineer from New York as far south as Richmond. In order to become qualified, my father walked the tracks (among other things) in places like Washington in order to pass the examination to qualify as an engineer in that particular area or over a specific route. My grandfather, after whom I am named, was also an engineer on steam locomotives, but he worked for the B&O Railroad. My father and my grandfather both started as firemen and later became qualified as engineers, however, they both had to wait until an engineer job became available before they were actually employed in that capacity.

Once my father became an engineer, he joined the Brotherhood of Locomotive Engineers. Back in the 1930's, the brotherhoods were a big deal in my family and all my parents' friends who were also working for the railroad belonged to one of the brotherhoods. Even after my parents moved to Camden and to Collingswood, all their friends were railroaders. Even when my father died in Camden, there were dozens upon dozens of railroaders who arrived from all over, i.e., New York, Washington, Baltimore, as well as South Jersey. It was a tough place to work when I was a boy. No vacations. My father and grandfather had to take time off to visit us at the seashore.

My father smoked heavily, more than a pack a day. He had a couple of eggs for breakfast each morning with thickly buttered bread. When I was a boy, we had four quarts of milk delivered each day and my father drank up to half of them. My father also had to have beef or pork every day. He didn't eat much chicken or fish except shellfish. He used to have one of the firemen bring him bags of oysters or clams on the engine from Ocean City, New Jersey. They were kept on ice in the cellar for instant shucking and slurping out of the shell. My father always tried to get your mother to swallow raw oysters or clams with little success.

My father also played basketball at the Kingsessing Recreation Center near where we lived. I have a picture of him and my Uncle Willis S. McCauley when they were members of the basketball team.[11]

From the time I was born until I was 20 I always lived in Philadelphia. First, we lived at 1631 S. 53rd Street and later at 1547 S. Lindenwood Street. Our house at 1547 S. Lindenwood Street was a two-story, three bedroom, row house in West Philadelphia. I remember my father figuring out that there were 57 children living on the street in 48 houses.

My bedroom was on the second floor in the rear. I had it all to myself. Tom was in the middle room. I had a single bed, Morris chair, antique chest, and closet. It was hot. No air conditioning. Cats used to fight all night in the summer in the back alleys and yards.

When I was young, it was a regular event to catch a mouse in the house several times a year. We set traps quite regularly. We never did stay overnight with a friend. There weren't many houses on Lindenwood Street that had any room for guests.

We were about the only family or one of the few families on our street to have a telephone in the 30's. Some of our close neighbors could use our telephone and put a nickel in the tin can by the telephone.

I only have vague memories of my maternal grandfather, Thomas McCauley, walking on his crutches as he only had one leg. I recall my other grandfather, William Scott Chambers, doing a tap dance and a soft shoe dance on his 77th birthday. Regarding my grandmother, I remember that in my early youth my mother suffered a complicated miscarriage and surgery requiring a lengthy hospital stay. During that time, my brother lived with Aunt Marge McCauley Smith and I lived for about a month with my grandmother, Josephine Reitze Chambers. I always remembered this stay as a very pleasant experience. My grandparents 50th wedding anniversary was just after the war. They had an open house all day long and people stopped by well into the night.

I only had one aunt and her name was Margaret McCauley Smith. My brother and I were very fond of her. We called her Aunt Marge. She was amusing and nice. Quite funny, really, though often unintentionally. She lived on the next street to us (1606 S. 53rd Street) and we saw her often. My mother was living with Aunt Marge when Aunt Marge died at home on 53rd Street.

I only had one uncle and his name was Willis Skillman McCauley. He and his family lived on the same street with us. He owned a 1929 Ford Model A. During the 1930's, we took many Sunday afternoon drives which was the custom in those days. Our first car was a 1936 Plymouth.

My father's only sister, Lucy Chambers Thompson, (mother of Josephine Thompson Marshall), unfortunately, died in 1918 so I never knew her.

GROWING UP ON LINDENWOOD STREET

When we were children, I remember that my cousin, Josephine Thompson, used to ride me around the neighborhood on the back of her bike. She had a small cushion for me to sit on over the rear fender of her bike. Neither my brother nor I ever had a bike (small tricycles, yes). My mother never approved of them. She felt they were dangerous in the city and that was that.

I also remember that I rode medium-sized ponies a great deal when I was a kid. A stable near me took the ponies out to sell rides in the neighborhoods. My brother and I and a few other kids would ride the ponies with the owners when they went to sell the rides and we would also walk the ponies with the little kids in the saddles. We didn't get paid for any of this work. The ponies were mostly from Chincoteague with a few Shetlands thrown in.

When I was seven and my brother was five, my father put us in a small open cockpit biplane that landed on the beach at Wildwood Crest. When we returned he put Josephine on. The airplane had two cockpits. The rear one for the pilot and the front one was for the passenger or two kids. When we got back to the apartment my mother and my grandmother gave my father Hell. This was a big adventure in 1928.

Whenever we got in trouble my mother would come after us and wack us with the first thing she could grab, frying pan, stick, switch. I bagged school occasionally and usually got caught. Punishment was fairly severe. I was usually restricted to the house for a week or more.

When I was born, Woodrow Wilson was the President. He only had one month left in his term. After that, Warren Harding was President. My mother was a staunch Republican. My father never said much about politics, but I know he voted for FDR in 1936. The same with my grandparents. The first presidential election in which I voted was in 1948 when I voted for Harry Truman. I was 27 years old at the time. Over the years, I saw three presidents, Roosevelt, Eisenhower, and Nixon. I also sat at a table for four with Vice President Hubert Humphrey in Kuala Lumpur, Malaysia, at a small lunch at the U.S. Embassy. In 1945, I did see one big shot general at his peak and that was General Douglas MacArthur. I saw him in Tokyo leaving a building where he stayed and getting into his command car to go to his headquarters. This was shortly after the occupation began. Strangely, as this was a daily occurrence, some Japanese always stood across the street to see the great man. The most famous person I ever met as a child was probably Grace Kelly's father, John B. Kelly, who was running for mayor.

When I was a child, I can remember a number of snow storms closing down Lindenwood Street to traffic. I also have vivid memories of the draft horses falling on the ice and snow. When we were children, everyone had a sled including my brother and me. We also built snowmen. We used pieces of coal for the face and sticks for the arms. I rarely went ice skating in the winter, but I did have a leg go through the ice up to my thigh. The temperature was two degrees and I had to walk 2 miles or more to get home. While the snow was often deep, at least for children, the schools were seldom closed. The schools were close and everyone walked to school. The main streets with trolley cars were cleared by trolley car plows, but otherwise there were no plows. The side streets remained partially blocked except for a center opening made by neighbors for horse drawn delivery of milk and bread and pick up wagons for garbage, ashes, and trash.

My favorite meal as a child was hot cakes and sausage for any meal. Since my father was often away, my brother and I had this often for supper. Strange as it may seem, I always remember supper at 5:00 PM with my brother and mother. In fact, the number one curfew was to be home for supper at 5:00 PM. No excuses. When we were younger we were not allowed out after dark. As we got older, my mother changed the rules from time to time, but they were strict. We always had a good dessert. My father was not often home for supper when we were kids. The only type of food I can remember making was scrambled eggs and scrapple.

How we spent our Saturdays during the school year depended on the season. We played baseball or football (no basketball). We also played hockey or skated long distances all over West Philadelphia. In fact, Tom and I both had roller skates and roamed all over southwest Philadelphia and played hockey on the street. I recall my mother (on a dare I guess) putting on my roller skates and skating up and down the street with the boys. She was a big hit. We walked and roamed everywhere. We also explored undeveloped areas and swampy wetlands (meadows) along the Pennsylvania Railroad.

When we were kids, it was customary for every boy to tie a string around a loose tooth and walk around with the string hanging down until he got the courage to yank the tooth out.

My favorite movies were the Saturday afternoon serials with cowboys Buck Jones, Tim McCoy, Tom Tyler. In fact, my favorite movie stars where the cowboys Tim McCoy and Tom Tyler. We also saw Dracula several times and my cousin, Skillman, always ducked under the seat in the spooky parts. The scary movies of the time - Dracula, The Phantom of the Opera, The Terror, Frankenstein, etc., used to keep me awake at night. As a small boy I was somewhat afraid of the dark when going to bed. I think it was the spooky movies. These scary movies were all the vogue in the 30's and all the kids went to the movies and got scared to death.

In the 1930's (first half), we always played cowboys and Indians and chased each other all over. Every kid had a cap pistol and the better ones had repeaters with a roll of caps. The fancy automatic pistols cost as much as 25 cents and a roll of caps was 2 cents.

We didn't have television when I was a child. I liked the radio serials such as Jack Armstrong, The All American Boy, H Bar O Ranch cowboy stories and Captain Diamond sea stories. Captain Diamond was a lighthouse keeper, retired from the sea, and he told sea stories. His sponsor was Diamond Crystal Shaker Salt. My family's favorite radio program was Amos and Andy. Jack Armstrong and The Shadow were favorites for Tom and me. Since there was no television, we also played Parcheesi, Chinese checkers, etc., and card games, and jig saw puzzles.

As a child I can remember singing "Old Mac Donald Had a Farm". I also vaguely remember, Tom and me in the bath tub with small boat, etc. I read a series of books in about Fourth Grade. They were called Bomba, the Jungle Boy. I thought they were neat. My favorite book was Treasure Island by Robert L. Stevenson.

Ice cream cones in the late 20's and the 30's were 5 cents. A big double dip cone was a dime. All loose candy was one cent. Baby Ruths, Hershey Bars, and the like were a nickel.

Everybody made chocolate fudge. It was a favorite snack that you made at home. Brownies were not invented yet, at least not in Philadelphia. As I remember, our favorite store when we were kids was Woolworth's Five and Ten Cent Store. Today, kids hang out at the mall.

We never had a swing when I was a kid because there really weren't any trees in our Philadelphia neighborhood capable of supporting a swing. Nor were there too many tree houses in Philadelphia. In fact, there were no trees or leaves to burn on Lindenwood Street. There were trees on Yocum Street where my grandparents' lived. Leaf burning was a regular event by the adults for the most part. Instead, when we were children, we used to build "bunks" of some sort in back yards or in vacant lots. We built the "bunks" in vacant lots out of 5 gal. cans, wood, stones, etc.

I learned to swim along with all the other kids in the pool at the Kingsessing Recreation Center. We usually went swimming at the public pool or at the shore at Wildwood. But, every summer some of the boys went swimming in a swampy lake out along the Pennsylvania Railroad tracks. We hitch hiked with regularity. While in high school and possibly before, we used to hitch hike out Woodland Avenue to Delaware County through Darby, then down U.S. Route Thirteen toward Chester to go swimming in a quarry flooded by rain and springs. It was very clear and deep. My longest hitch hiking trip was from Philadelphia to Washington on a Memorial Day weekend to see the festivities. I did this while I was a cadet on the Schoolship. I saw President Roosevelt at Arlington. Once, three other kids and I walked at least 8 miles round trip to the Philadelphia airport to see the airplanes come in. It turned out to be an all day affair and our parents were wild looking for us.

My father frequently made small toys, etc., for me and he made a stretching frame for drying rabbit and squirrel skins. My father and cousin, Augie Muller were avid small game hunters - ducks, pheasants, rabbits, squirrels, etc. and I went a few times. My mother dutifully cooked up the prizes and we all ate it for dinner. Fred Queroli, Augie Muller and my father used to go rabbit hunting together in Delaware County. My father also went duck hunting in Tinicum near the airport. The double barreled shotgun that belonged to my father was given to him by William Patton (my mother's first cousin, once removed). King, our dog, was an English Setter bird dog, but he was gun shy so he couldn't be used for hunting. The men told my father that King should be shot as he wasn't any good for hunting, but my father wouldn't do it. King stayed at home from then on. He got distemper and had to be put to sleep. I took him to the vet to be "put down" because no one else would do it. He was a big, lovable dog who used to sit on my mother's lap.

As a child, my mother would take us and other kids living on the street on a long walk through the lots and up on the bank overlooking the main line (New York to Washington) of the Pennsylvania Railroad. She had it timed so that in a few minutes the "Congressional Limited" came steaming past at full speed on its way to Washington with my father waving from the locomotive cab. I was a big shot.

When I was in grammar school, a little girl and a little boy died of disease and two boys were killed in accidents. They all lived on or just off 53rd Street. The deaths affected not only me, but most of the other kids also.

I went fishing a few times when I was a kid, but never liked it much. Occasionally, we would catch tadpoles and put them in fish tanks and try to raise frogs. It never worked except for one time. We also used to catch garter snakes (young ones about 10 in. or so). Cartons or bowls were used to hold them. It was a big deal to take them to school in your pocket to scare the girls.

MY TEENAGE YEARS

When Tom and I went to junior high school, my father gave us 25 cents every two weeks when he got paid. The amount increased slowly as we got older. Although we didn't earn our allowance, we worked around the house scrubbing the kitchen floor, vacuuming, etc., but there was seldom any pay involved. My chores as a child were always to scrub the kitchen floor and wash the windows on the outside. We put out trash and ashes (very heavy) when my father wasn't home. We did not have outside chores except cleaning the dog dirt from the backyard. My father did all the painting and washed the car. Tom and I did all the food shopping once we entered junior high school. Before that shopping was limited to the deli for ham, cheese, Campbell's soup, and the like. My mother bought the major meats - turkey, roast beef, leg of lamb, etc. Shopping was a long walk to the store and loads were heavy.

Traveling carnivals were still the vogue in the 1930's and about three came through every summer and put up tents and stands on a vacant lot for a week or so. There were all the usual rides - ferris wheels, flying swings, crack the whip, merry go rounds, spinning plates, etc. They cost 5 cents and 10 cents a ride. Hot dogs were a nickel.

The strangest thing I ever saw in the sky was a total eclipse of the sun (or nearly so) in Philadelphia about 1934. Everyone was on edge for weeks before the big event.

My favorite time of year when I was a kid was always summer. No school. And maybe January or any time it snowed. Even though summer was my favorite time of year, heat waves were regular every summer in Philadelphia. In row houses with windows only on the front and back and no air-conditioning it was tough to sleep. When we were young, we would get under the hose in the backyard to stay cool. Also, in Philadelphia, the fire hydrant, which was turned on and off all summer, substituted for the suburban sprinkler of later years as a means of keeping cool. As I recall lightning and thunder storms were frequent and severe in Philadelphia in the summer. At least it seems so to me. All the kids ran home in any case.

As a boy, all our vacations were the same, but just what we wanted. My mother, my grandmother, Josephine, Tom, and I went to Wildwood for a month. In fact, we spent most of August through Labor Day at Wildwood, New Jersey. My father and grandfather came down when they could. Also, my mother, Tom, and I went to Queroli's house in Sea Isle City, New Jersey, for a week or less. As I recall, my father and Fred Queroli came down for a few days.

When I was a kid, we didn't have best school chums. When we left school for the day we no longer saw our classmates. Our life revolved around the neighborhood especially Lindenwood Street where about 60 children lived. They were your friends and playmates. Very few best chums. Everybody was just called Joe, Marty, Eddie, Frank, and Bill, etc. One kid on our street was called Beezer and the Jewish kid on the next street was called Jewky Greenberg and another was called Bushie Stein. A boy in the next street was named Donald Duckworth. Unfortunately, Walt Disney came out about then with Mickey Mouse and Donald Duck. The poor kid was always known as Donald Duck. We didn't seem to have a best friend in those days. However, I was close to Jim Cosgrove who lived across the street and with Melvin Bee (called Beezer). Incidentally, Beezer was wounded in the Marine Corps and Jim was hurt in a kamikaze attack off the Philippines in World War II. Neither one seriously.

There was always a war around during my youth - Italy invading Ethiopia and parts of other north African countries, Japan invading north China and Shanghai, and Hitler invading the Saar, Sudatenland, and Austria - all ending up with World War II starting in 1939.

When I was a kid, the usual thing was to buy a kite once. When the paper became torn you re-papered the kite with newspaper or something lighter if you could find it. We all had hundreds of feet of string on a stick. It was a big deal.

Our neighborhood was over 2 miles from the Catholic and the public high schools so no one went out for after school football, etc. The practice fields were even further away. So I did not participate in high school sports. We had local organized and pickup teams and played at a local recreation center called Kingsessing. I played football for the Kingsessing Hawks in 1936. I played tackle and end. We were good.

I could and can still play the harmonica. We had a harmonica band at Sunday School for a couple of years. I was a member of the band. I still have my harmonica (mouth organ) and part of my stamp collection. In fact, my foreign stamp collection was probably my most prized possession when I was young. I was an avid stamp collector as a kid as were many other boys. Procter and Gamble had a weekly radio show where Captain Tim, a world traveler, told worldwide adventure stories about distant lands. You could get all sorts of foreign stamps by sending in Ivory Soap wrappers. We used to go through other people's trash every week looking for Ivory Soap wrappers.

My best talent was probably carpentry and drawing (copying pictures). As an adult, my favorite pastimes include wood working and birding.

MY SOCIAL LIFE

Regarding girlfriends, I remember that my first girlfriend was Peggy Pursley. She was fourteen and so was I. As I remember, there were no festivities at our school for Valentine's day. My first real date was in high school when I took Dorothy Keene to the movies. My father gave me a dollar which covered all expenses for the theater and the food.

When I was in high school, we "hung out" on the corner. A few years before the war, jukebox dance places sprang up in vacant stores. They had booths, ice cream and soda, pastry, etc., no liquor. The Catholic churches held dances every Friday night, jukeboxes and big band records. Straight dancing and jitter bugging were very big.

My first dance was the eighth grade dance in junior high school (A.H. Shaw). My next door neighbor, Dorothy Stetler, taught me to dance and we practiced in her house all week. She wanted to be sure she had someone to dance with in case no one else asked her. The dance was in the gym after school.

One big problem I had in high school was who to ask to my prom and finally all the girls were taken, at least in my neighborhood.

As I said, I did not go to my high school prom due to the lack of a suitable date. But I went to the West Catholic Prom with Virginia Toner who invited me. I also went to Halahan Catholic Girls high school with Florence Miller who invited me.

When I was growing up "On the Isle of Capri" and Beer Barrel Polka were big deals and, of course, the big bands were coming in strong. Bing Crosby was "in" to all ages. There were not too many singing groups (Ink Spots, Andrews Sisters) as this was the era of the big band with soloists. My favorites were probably Glenn Miller and Larry Clinton. There were any number of female vocalists that I liked in the late 30's and during the war - Vera Lynn, Jo Stafford, Frances Lansford, Dinah Shore. There were two dances in my youth, jitter bug and what we called slow dances. Jitter bug was very popular, but hard to do well. Slow dancing was my forte. Most of the big band numbers that are remembered today and that are sort of classics were slow dance type.

MY SCHOOL LIFE

The best advice my mother gave me was to finish high school and stay away from drink.

I went to Benjamin B. Comegy from first to sixth. I attended Anna Howard Shaw junior high school from seventh to ninth and I went to West Philadelphia high school. My cousin, Josephine, also graduated from the same three schools, but my brother graduated from John Bartrum high school which opened shortly after I graduated from high school. By the way, Bartrum was located at 70th and Elmwood, if I remember correctly, and we lived at 53rd and

Woodland. That was a long walk in those days before there were school buses. Usually we wore a white shirt and knit tie to school and, if classes were cold, we wore a sweater. We wore knickers until sometime in junior high school and then long pants through high school.

I can't seem to remember even one special custom at any of these schools. I think our school colors were maroon and white in Comegy and Shaw. In high school the colors were orange and blue. There were no school mascots. As for cheerleaders in high school, the girls wore white culottes and a sweater with orange and blue trim. The boys wore the same sweater with slacks. I cannot remember any of the high school cheers, but we sing the school song whenever we meet at a reunion.

The only thing I remember about my first day at school was walking with some other kids about three blocks to Benjamin B. Comegy grammar school. No parents were involved. School was from 8:45 AM to Noon. We walked home for lunch and then had school from 1:20 PM to 3:30 PM. At recess we played running games, tag, etc. There was no playground equipment at the school. Fortunately, my parents never made us wear anything stupid to school except overshoes when it snowed which wasn't very cool.

We walked to and from school, grades one through twelve, rain, shine, or snow, zero degrees to 100 degrees F. It would've been a tough job with my mother to pretend to be sick as an excuse to stay home from school.

In grammar school, I remember Mrs. Shields (a tall woman in gray) was the principal in my first few years. She, at times, used to swing through the little boys room (which was large) at recess time to shoo all the kids out who were playing in there.

One didn't play tricks on teachers in Philadelphia in the 1930's. Unfortunately, in our school there were always one or two children with an IQ of about 80. In West Philadelphia there was a school named Paul Revere which was for wild kids. I knew several kids who were transferred to the "Riding Academy" as it was affectionately called.

I don't remember the first time I smoked. All the boys in grammar school (fifth and sixth grade) used to shoot butts or get one of the older kids to buy a cigarette for one cent at Dunoff's Deli.

In Philadelphia we were graded E for excellent; G for good; F for fair; P for poor; VP for very poor. I never got a poor or a very poor. My favorite subjects at school were math and history probably because they were interesting to me and therefore easy. My least favorite subject was English. I had plenty of homework, but I got most of it done at lunch or in study hall. I was sorry later that I didn't pay more attention. I didn't learn to write well until I went to college where a paper was due every week for two years in either history or English. If I were to return to my youth, maybe I would study more in school.

There were 730 students in my high school class when we graduated in June 1939. The class that graduated in February 1939 was a bit smaller. Each year had two classes - A and B. The total school held about 6,000 students. Yes, we had portable classrooms. They were called shacks. My high school was crowded. We went to school in shifts - 8:45 AM - 2:15 PM; 9:30 AM - 3:00 PM; 10:15 AM - 3:45 PM

I was the school champ in chess for two years in junior high school. I won a tournament once in high school and then retired. In high school I wished I could have been a good gymnast. While I was strong and could do push ups and chin ups, climb ropes, etc., I was not good on gym equipment.

My high school graduation exercises were held in the Academy of Music located at Broad and Locust. It was very posh - elegant. It is still the home of the Philadelphia symphony and opera. I graduated from West Philadelphia high school in June 1939. I don't recall any school from first through college having a homecoming. My high school class of 1939 still holds annual reunions. I went to the 60th reunion in June 1999 in Bala Cynwyd, Pennsylvania.

I graduated from the Pennsylvania Maritime Academy (Schoolship Annapolis) in September 1941. Two of the boys in my class, Wallace "Wally" Robert Horton, 3rd Engineer on the Atlantic Sun (d. 02/17/43) and Harry Arthur Wolfe, 3rd Mate on the Louise Lykes (01/09/43) were lost at sea during World War II. I knew them both very well.

OUR PETS

We had lots of pets when we were children, dogs, cats, Guinea pigs, birds, fish, ducks, etc., but the best pet by far was a black-and-white English Setter named King who went everywhere with us and all the gang. There is a picture of my brother, Tom, and the Cosgrove boys with our dog, King, at a swamp called "W" along the railroad tracks in West Philadelphia below 58th and Woodland. My father and all of us tried to raise tropical fish and canaries with a fair degree of success.

SUMMER CAMP

The only summer camp I had was Citizens Military Training Camp (CMTC). First was 30 days infantry training at Fort Meade, Maryland, in 1938 and second was 30 days in field artillery at Fort Hoyle, Maryland, in 1939.

I was never actually in the armed forces, but I, Tom, and other boys from the neighborhood went to the Citizens Military Training Camp (CMTC) during summers in high school. The minimum age was seventeen years, but many of the boys were sixteen years old and my brother, Tom, got in at fifteen, somehow. Tom served in the Sixth Horse Drawn Field Artillery at Fort Hoyle, Maryland, and in the Third U.S. Cavalry at Fort Belvoir, Virginia. I served in the 34th Infantry at Fort Meade, Maryland, and in the Sixth Field Artillery at Fort Hoyle.

Except at training camp when we slept in tents, we never slept under the stars. It really wasn't done in our area. We tried a few times in the backyard, but mosquitoes were too much. As a kid, we used to build fires in the open field areas, but I never liked roasted hot dogs or marshmallows. I do now.

MY JOBS AS A KID

As a kid, my first job was helper on a laundry truck, picking up and delivering laundry. I also had a newspaper route delivering the afternoon edition of the *Philadelphia Public Ledger*. I gave the route to my cousin, Skillman McCauley, when I was put on the third shift in the tenth grade of high school which didn't let out until 3:45 PM which was too late to walk 3 miles to pick up the papers. The usual pay was about a dollar a day on the laundry truck plus lunch in a diner. Serving newspapers was six days a week plus collecting on Saturday morning. Newspapers were 2 cents each or 12 cents per week. When I collected 12 cents from each customer on Saturday, I got to keep 3 cents, so with 30 customers I usually made 90 cents take home pay.

MY MEDICAL MALADIES

I don't remember ever breaking any bones as a child except that I cracked my nose from football. I never needed any stitches except for the operation on my foot. When I was a child, I had pneumonia, chicken pox, and whopping cough all at the same time. I hardly remember it, but apparently I was very sick. One day when I was little while I was at my Aunt Marge's house, I remember that I got my right ring finger caught in the door. I recall that my mother pulled me in a wagon to 52nd and Chester to visit Dr. Steward. Also, my mother gave us a big bottle of citrate of magnesia every month to clean the poisons out of our body. Other than that, I don't remember much about seeing a doctor or dentist except that in March 1942 I was called to active service in the U.S. Naval Reserve and failed to pass a physical exam because of a heart murmur.

By far my biggest physical problem was my bad right leg. The foot was limp and the leg was skinny. This was a terrible embarrassment in junior and senior high school. Probably most people never realized it, but I sure did. My right arm was also affected and the lack of power and dexterity in the arm prevented me from playing golf or batting a baseball well. There are three pictures of me taken at the Lulu Temple (pre-Shriners Hospital) which was located on Broad Street. These pictures were taken prior to my operation to lengthen my Achilles tendon. The operation took place in 1926. I was in the Shriners Hospital for seven months on Roosevelt Boulevard in North Philadelphia.

I had poison ivy many times as a boy. Sometimes all over my body. So did Tom and many other kids. Other than that, I was never really home sick except when I went into the Shriners Hospital at age six for seven months. I only had visitors on Sunday and not every week. The worst part was the first ten days when each child was quarantined to prevent the spread of childhood diseases. Even so, I eventually got whopping cough, chicken pox, and pneumonia all at once.

BIRTHDAYS AND SPECIAL EVENTS

Birthdays were not a big event when we lived on Lindenwood Street. My mother always baked a cake and Breyers ice cream was served with the Cosgrove boys across the street sometimes invited. Tom and I always had a homemade cake every year until we left home. I never remember a store bought cake. No party as such. My mother never really made special gifts for us except food and pastries.

I went to Sunday School every Sunday until I was 20. I never missed in sixteen years. I don't know where the medals are now.[12] Although my brother and I were baptized at Tabor Presbyterian Church in South Philadelphia, we attended the First United Presbyterian Church at 52nd and Chester Avenue.[13] My mother made the decision to switch churches when we were old enough to go to Sunday School as the First United Presbyterian Church was within walking distance of our house.

Movies were allowed to open on Sunday in Philadelphia about 1935, but we were never allowed to go. We could watch sand lot ball games (baseball and football), but we were not allowed to play. Sunday was not a big day. We were not allowed to swim on Sunday either. Since Tom and I never missed a Sunday in fifteen years, there were not many special memories of going to church. The annual Sunday School picnic was the event of the year. My mother always took the Cosgrove boys from across the street and we had a ball swimming, rock climbing, and all sorts of races plus food. Melvin Bee (Beezer) and I always won the three legged race. The picnics were held at Castle Rock, Pennsylvania or at Glen Rock, New Jersey. Once, Tom and I participated in a Tom Thumb Wedding.[14] He was the best man and I was an usher. It was a full dress affair. The church had occasional covered dish socials, but they were mainly for adults.

Being from the wrong county in Ireland, St. Patrick's Day was not a big event in our lives.

Easter was quite a religious holiday in our house and in our neighborhood. Sunday School and church, of course, and you kept your Sunday best clothes on until late in the day.

May Day was not a big deal on Lindenwood Street. However, it just occurred to me that in the early 30's when I was in B.B. Comegy School, each class had a May Pole. The girls walked around the pole in opposite directions, weaving in and out, with long multi-colored ribbons.

On Mother's Day, Tom and I wore a red carnation to Sunday School and kept our Sunday clothes on all day.

Memorial Day was usually spent at Mount Moriah Cemetery. All the family went with flowers, etc., to decorate the graves. It was still called Decoration Day by most people. Soldiers fired over the various veterans grave areas. It was a day long affair including walking out and back. When I was in the Boys Brigade, we participated in a big Memorial Day Parade on Broad Street - uniforms, rifles, and all. I remember that one time Tom and I were lined up to go tent camping for two weeks with the Boys Brigade. We were packed and waiting to be picked up on Sunday, but when the station wagon arrived we were told the camp was completely washed out the night before in the rain storm.

On Independence Day, there was the annual parade for kids starting at Comegy School, then Mitchell School, and then Most Blessed Sacrament, and then on to Kingsessing Recreation Center for games and races and free ice cream. Fire crackers were illegal in Philadelphia. They were also illegal with my mother so that was that. Fire crackers were available in Delaware County so there were lots of bangs going off. A big fireworks display was given in Clarks Park at 45th and Kingsessing on the fourth of July night which we all attended. The fourth of July was a big event in the 30's with parades and fireworks, etc. I think the holidays were used to keep the natives from becoming restless during the Great Depression.

On Halloween, we would dress in a costume and go to all the houses in the neighborhood looking for nuts and fruit. There was no candy given out in those days.

Our only family reunions when I was a child were get-togethers on Thanksgiving and Christmas. Christmas was my favorite holiday - of course. Other holidays were non-events for me for the most part. Our big toy was erector sets and electric trains which were only brought out for a month at Christmas.

When I was young, Thanksgiving was always the same. Roast turkey, stuffing, gravy, homemade cranberry sauce, vegetables, candied sweet potatoes, mashed potatoes, cauliflower au gratin, peas, and creamed onions. We also had homemade pumpkin pie and minced meat pie well laced with whiskey. The guests were my grandparents, the Smiths, and sometimes Willis McCauley's family. Dinner was served only after the Pennsylvania - Cornell football game (on the radio) was finished about 5:00 PM.

I was in several Christmas pageants at Sunday School and church. When I was young, it was the custom to put up the Christmas tree on Christmas Eve day not a week ahead of time as is done today. We decorated the tree with the usual things, balls and tinsel plus an occasional other small ornament. We also hung Christmas stockings. The best Christmas presents we ever received were new units for our large electric train system. My father was a toy train buff. When we were high school age we went to church on Christmas Eve, but not as children. Sometime in the early 1930's, our dog (King) decided to chase the cat who escaped into the living room at full speed and scrambled up the newly trimmed Christmas tree with such vigor that the tree tipped over.

OUR AUTOMOBILES

Our family's first car was a four door 1936 Plymouth. I was fifteen and Tom was thirteen. I don't recall playing any games while riding in the car. In fact, I don't recall any trips except to Delaware County to visit Augie Muller or a very occasional trip to Liberty Grove, Maryland, to visit Uncle John Smith's family.

Our first car cost $700.00 (black). The money came from a $900.00 World War I veterans bonus which was due in 20 years, but Roosevelt had Congress pay it in 1936 to "prime the pump" during the depression. Dad taught me to drive in 1937 when I became sixteen.

My first car was the same 1936 Plymouth given to your mother and me in 1947 by my father. You, your mother, and I came down and picked up the car in Collingswood and drove to Cambridge (MIT) in September 1947. That was a long way to go in that car. We stopped a day or two in Bridgeport, Connecticut, with Fran and Helen Fagan.

GOING TO SEA

When I was a kid, the old frigate U.S.S. Constitution was towed up and down the east coast to raise money for repairs. The schools collected pennies from the students. Kids were admitted free to the ship. That's when I fell in love with ships. The ship was eventually moored in Boston as a museum piece.

A person who had a big influence on my life was a neighbor of ours named Bill Smith (born in Ireland) who was a few years older than me. He went to sea as a merchant seaman and helped solidify my desire to go to sea. He started as an ordinary seaman and was sailing as a Mate during World War II. He was never a Cadet. He came up through the Hause Pipe as they say or out of the foc's'le.

I always wanted to go to sea and be a sailor - travel all over the world. A distant second choice was to be a fireman on the railroad. My cousin Skillman recently told me that Tom and I were considered lucky kids because my father shoveled coal on the railroad. A real man.

Upon graduation from high school in 1939, I went to the Pennsylvania State Nautical School (also known as the Pennsylvania Maritime Academy for a few years after World War II until it was closed down).[15] I lived on the Schoolship Annapolis for two years because I wanted a career in the U.S. Merchant Marine.[16] We slept in hammocks. I went home on the weekend with my laundry. I took training cruises on the Schoolship Seneca, the U.S.S. Pyro, and the U.S.S. Omaha. I graduated October 24, 1941.

I received my original Third Mates License in October 1941 from the Steamboat Inspection Service (or something similar), a bureau of the Department of Commerce. Sometime after the war started, the merchant ship inspection and licensing function was taken over by the

U.S. Coast Guard where it remains today. Thus, I received my Second Mates and Chief Mates Licenses from the U.S. Coast Guard. I obtained a license to sail as Master of Ships of any gross tons upon oceans in February 1945. I sailed as a Deck Officer from November 1941 to September 1949.

My original Seaman's Certificate of Identification was issued June 21, 1939, at Philadelphia and was numbered Z-129718. It went down with the S.S. Steel Worker during World War II. A replacement Certificate of Identification was issued to me at Philadelphia on August 14, 1942. It was numbered Z-129718-D1.

I was on my first trip as a Junior Third Mate on the S.S. Steelmaker en route from Panama to Honolulu when the war started. I arrived in Honolulu on December 15, 1941. While eating breakfast before going on 8 to 12 bridge watch, the Captain came into the Officers' Salon and announced the receipt of a radio message from the U.S. Navy San Francisco that Japan attacked Pearl Harbor a few hours earlier and we were to follow sealed orders the Captain had received at Panama.

I signed foreign articles to serve as Third Mate on the S.S. Steel Worker belonging to the Isthmian Steamship Company on March 26, 1942, at Philadelphia. The S.S. Steel Worker sailed from Philadelphia to Murmansk, Russia, via Halifax (Nova Scotia), Greenock (Scotland), Reykjavik (Iceland) and Hvalfjord (Iceland). I think we lost eight ships in the north bound crossing of the convoy.[17] Our ship was sunk by enemy action (possibly a mine) while navigating through the Kola Inlet on June 3.[18] I was rescued from a life boat by a British corvette and transferred on June 4 to the S.S. Alcoa Cadet. The S.S. Alcoa Cadet was sunk off the Kola Inlet on June 21.[19] I was rescued from a raft by a Russian patrol craft and transferred to a Russian military barracks across the river from Murmansk on June 21/22. I remember that I got my first wrist watch when I graduated from high school. It went down with the S.S. Steel Worker when it sank on June 3, 1942 off Kola Inlet, North Russia.

On June 27, I and some other surviving crew members were transferred from the Russian military barracks to the S.S. American Press for transportation in a south bound convoy to Hoboken, New Jersey, via Iceland. My notes say: July 5 - 9 PM off west coast of Iceland - submarine attack, 6 ships sunk. One ship hit and made the port of Reykjavik.[20] Our captain on the S.S. American Press always questioned the attack and thought we may have hit a mine field as all the ships went up almost at the same time. In any case, the convoy scattered and we turned about and headed north for the town of Akureyi in a fjord on the north coast of Iceland. A Certificate of Discharge was issued to me by the Shipping Commissioner on August 3, in New York, when I returned to the United States.

During WW II, I was Third Mate on the SS Robin Sherwood and on December 30, 1942, we sailed from New York destined for the Panama Canal. Upon clearing the canal we took a circuitous route from Balboa, Canal Zone to Fremantle in Western Australia. The voyage from Balboa to Fremantle took 28 days with no land or ships sighted. It was one long voyage. In order to avoid any contact with the Japanese we also sailed an indirect route from Fremantle to the Persian Gulf where we discharged military supplies in several Iranian ports for further transport overland to Russia. After we sailed from the Persian Gulf about June 1, 1943, we proceeded south along the east coast of Africa and called at Mombasa, Kenya; Dar Es Salaam, Tanganyika (now known as Tanzania); and Beira in Mozambique to load commercial cargo. It was while we were in Dar Es Salaam that I bought three black elephants with ivory tusks.[21] We then sailed around South Africa first stopping at Durban before we headed across the South Atlantic to Rio de Janeiro. From there we sailed to New York for a total of 36,000 miles for the round the world trip from New York to New York.

I remember V.J. (Victory Japan) Day. I was appointed as Master of my first ship, the S.S. Thomas J. Walsh, on May 24, 1945, after which we embarked on a long voyage from Charleston, South Carolina, with calls at Gibraltar and various ports in Italy, France, Panama, and the Philippines. We were en-route from Marseille, France, to San Fernando-Lingayen Gulf in the Philippines when the atomic bomb was dropped. I was in Japan by October 1945 and bought a string of pearls for your mother. In a wedding picture, she is wearing the pearls.

After the end of World War II, I returned from Japan and paid off as Captain of the S.S. Thomas J. Walsh on January 18, 1946, in Norfolk, Virginia. During World War II, I earned the following American medals award by the United States Government: World War II 1941-1945; Mediterranean Middle-East War Zone; Pacific War Zone; Atlantic War Zone; and Enemy Action with Two Stars.[22] Fifty years after the end of the war, I was also awarded the Commemorative Medal "The Fiftieth Anniversary of the Victory in the Great Patriotic War (World War II)" by President Boris Yeltsin, the Russian Government, and the entire Russian people. This Russian medal was awarded in recognition of courage and personal contribution to the Allied support of Russia during her fight for freedom against Germany.

I applied to MIT for acceptance in the Naval Architecture Department which I had planned for a year.[23] Your mother and I married on January 26, 1946. We honeymooned in New York, Baltimore, and Bermuda. We returned to Princeton in late February. A letter had arrived from MIT instructing me to take the SAT and college boards in comprehensive math, chemistry, and physics. I engaged a tutor from the Hun School (a science professor) recommended by your grandmother to tutor me for three hours a week during March. I took the four exams in the first week or so of April. Then, I signed on the S.S. Sea Witch as Chief Mate on April 15, 1946. I was transferred to the S.S. Kenyon L. Butterfield as Master on May 1 and sailed for Europe. Your mother met me in New York at the end of June with the acceptance letter from MIT. I made one more trip to Europe and paid off on August 20, finished the paperwork, and off we went to Boston by train. Upon arriving in Boston we went to MIT for help in finding lodging. We found a furnished room with Mr. Clarenden Faulkner at 78 Grafton Street in Arlington, Massachusetts. We also had kitchen privileges including a coal oil stove and half the refrigerator. We lived on the second floor.

COURTSHIP AND MARRIAGE

I met your mother in early February 1944 in New York on a blind date set up by Victor E. Tyson who was Second Mate on the S.S. Charles J. Folger (I was Chief Mate) and his girlfriend (later his wife) Vivian Semasko who worked with your mother as a buyer for Yards Department Store in Trenton, New Jersey.

Vic and Vivian, your mother and I went to see "Oklahoma" in New York and then we went to Shines Restaurant which was famous for their late night ham and eggs. After eating, your mother became violently ill. We put Vivian and your mother in my hotel room and Victor and I went back to our ship.

Your mother was able to come into New York whenever my ship came in. It was an exciting time. The war was raging at its height in Europe and in the Pacific. New York was wild. It was eat, drink, and be merry for tomorrow you never knew what. We got along well and did it up big with Vivian and Vic (who also later got married). Don't forget, young men were rare in those days and one phone call to your mother and Vivian in Princeton and they were on their way on a 50 mile train ride to New York.

In February 1945, your mother and Vivian were working as buyers for Franklin and Simon Department Store in New York and living with Bertha and Joe Carey in a small apartment in Bayside (Queens) New York.[24] Vacant apartments in New York were nil. Vic Tyson and I were staying over one night and I proposed marriage to your mother and it took her one second to say yes. We decided to make the wedding arrangements when I returned the next trip. I sailed on March 6, 1945, as Chief Mate on the S.S. Thomas J. Walsh from Baltimore to Naples, Civita Vecchia (Rome), and Oran, Algeria. In Italy I received a letter from your mother that her sister, Kathryn (Tootsie) had died March 30, 1945, and she wanted to postpone our wedding.

Upon my return to Charleston, South Carolina, on May 20, 1945, your mother came down to stay until I sailed a week later on my first trip as Master. Your grandmother said not to delay the wedding. We decided to get married six to eight weeks later when I returned. We sailed at the end of May for Naples, Catania, and Gallipoli, Italy. Since the Germans had surrendered in May, the powers that be decided to send us to Marseilles, France, to load an infantry division's equipment destined for the Philippines via the Panama Canal. Before our arrival in San Fernando on Luzon, the atomic bomb was dropped and Japan surrendered. We were directed to Tokyo Bay from Luzon and eventually we returned to Norfolk, Virginia, via Philadelphia, about January 15, 1946 - six months late for my wedding.

We were married on January 26, 1946, in the First Presbyterian Church (now called Nassau Presbyterian) in Princeton, New Jersey. I wore my maritime uniform. The minister was Dr. Frank Niles. My brother, Thomas Wallace Chambers, was the best man and Corinne Cameron was the maid of honor. Frances Murray was bridesmaid. Vivian Semasko who had introduced us was to be in the wedding, but she had married Vic Tyson and was well pregnant and couldn't fit into her bridesmaid dress.

It was a cold January day and the ground was snow covered from a snow fall the night before. After we were married and the reception was over we took a 10:00 PM train to New York. After a few days in New York at the Henry Hudson Hotel we went by train to Baltimore for two days while we waited for the departure of BOAC (British Overseas Airways Corporation) flying boat to Bermuda. The big seaplane "landed" in Hamilton Harbor. We stayed a week.

When we were first married, we stayed in Princeton with your grandmother Freda while I studied and took the college boards for MIT. I never heard of pizza until I was married. Tony Friel took us to the "Burg" in Trenton (Chambersburg where Little Italy was located). I only remember plain cheese. This was 1946. After the exams, I went back to sea on the S.S. Sea Witch (coast wise cruise) and then as Master on the S.S. Kenyon L. Butterfield for a trip to France and a second trip to London and Plymouth. Upon paying off the ship on August 20, 1946, we stayed with my parents in Philadelphia until early September when we took a train to Boston and college.

My job at the time I was married was Ships Officer, U.S. Merchant Marine.

THE EARLY YEARS OF MY MARRIAGE

One serious problem I faced during the early years of our marriage was getting my homework done with you screaming through the paper walls from the next room. Shopping was also a problem for the first two years we were at MIT because we had no car. We solved grocery shopping problems by walking with you in a carriage for one or 2 miles and sitting you on top of the bags of groceries for the return trip. We used the subway to go downtown or a trolley car.

We had two daughters in all. The first was you, Kathryn Judith Chambers, born March 26, 1947 in Boston, Massachusetts, at the Massachusetts General Hospital.[25] Our second child was your sister, Cynthia Scott Chambers, born March 5, 1953 in Havana, Cuba, at the Anglo American Hospital in the Vedado section of the city.[26]

When you were born we lived at our little house at 28 Westgate on a former ball field at MIT. We had no telephone and no car. On the evening of March 25, I called the doctor on a neighbor's telephone. He said to go to Massachusetts General. I took your mother (or rather the Barriers took us as we had no car) late in the evening about 10:00 PM. I stayed with your mother some hours when I was told that nothing was imminent so I could go home and they would call. I taxied home to sleep. About 7:00 AM on March 26 our back neighbor pounded on the door stating the hospital called and you were alive and well. Apparently, you were born at 6:43 A.M. I walked to Kendal Square and took a subway to Boston and saw you through the plate glass window in the nursery. When your mother awakened, I spoke with her for an hour or so and then took the subway back to school for a Noon quiz on Engineering Drawing and Design. Then I went back to the hospital by subway. Thomas R. Goethals was the doctor who delivered you. He was recommended by a Trenton MD. He was also supposed to be the Chief of Obstetrics at Harvard Medical School. You and your mother stayed in the hospital for ten days as was the custom back then.

You were named after your mother's sister who had died in an accident about two years before. The accident was a chemical explosion where she worked. We never really considered any other name for you. Your mother wanted to use her sister's name and I agreed completely.

Harry Truman was the president when you were born. As I said, you were born in the Massachusetts General Hospital in Boston. That hospital was (and still is) huge. Apparently, Baker Memorial Hospital (the facility in which you were actually born) and other buildings were all part of the whole. Massachusetts General was a teaching hospital for Harvard Medical School. Who owned that hospital is not clear to me. As I said previously, our home was at 28 Westgate, Cambridge, Massachusetts, where we lived in MIT married students housing.

As I mentioned, you were a noisy baby although healthy. When you and your mother came home from the hospital your grandmother Freda arrived to help. After about four days of arguments with your mother about how to handle a new born baby, your grandmother picked up and left for Princeton.

During the late 1940's at MIT, one of our neighbors in Westgate (the Dexters) had a New Year's Eve party where I ate and drank a bit to excess and was violently ill all night and all day (New Year's Day). Your mother and you were greatly amused as I hung over the toilet. The only other odd thing I can remember is that I was never bitten by a dog until I was an adult and going to MIT. A dog nipped me when jogging to school.

While I was at MIT, I did not attend classes during the summers of 1947, 1948, or 1949. During the summer of 1947, I was helping your mother with a new born baby (you), so I did not work. In the summer of 1948, I worked on the railroad as a fireman (coal heaver). The trains were taking tomatoes from Pennsylvania to the Campbell Soup Company near Camden, New Jersey. My father was working on the railroad at the time and helped me get the job. During the summer of 1949, I was at sea and made three trips to Europe as a relief mate on the S.S. Marine Shark.

I graduated from MIT on June 9, 1950. My first job after graduation was as Assistant Marine Superintendent with the Ward Line Steamship Company in New York City.

LIFE IN CUBA

We arrived in Cuba in December 1950. I do not remember the exact date, but it was on a Tuesday.[27] All Ward Line ships from New York arrived in Havana on Tuesday.[28] We had to establish residency in Cuba before the end of the year in order to avoid paying U.S. income taxes for the year 1951, i.e., you had to be out of the country for the full year to escape taxes.

All new American arrivals stayed at Miss Ross' Boarding House when they first came to Havana. It was located at Calle 3 and C in Vedado. It was just done. The company had made all the arrangements. That is where your mother met Daisy Gonzalez.[29],[30] She worked at Miss Ross' Boarding House and was in charge of the kitchen. Like all Cubans, they had a pig in the yard in late December to be eaten at Christmas. We had Christmas dinner at the home of Anne and Doug Singer. The other guests were Dr. Carlos Figuredo and his wife. He was Secretary of La Compañía Terminal Cubana Americana where I was going to work and handled all the paperwork for our permits to stay and work in Cuba. I often wondered what happened to him.

We moved from Miss Ross' Boarding House to an apartment in Miramar which was then located in the municipality of Marianao, just outside the City of Havana. The address was Calle 10, # 25 and it was about a block or so away from the Blanquita Theater. We moved to Calle 10 in Miramar probably in late January 1951. Our apartment in Miramar was unusual in that it had two floors with a marble staircase going up to the bedrooms. The maids' quarters were in the rear over the garages. It was there that we met the Browns who lived across the hall and the Joneses who lived downstairs. The Godinezes lived around the corner. Incidentally, Max Jones had lived at Miss Ross' house when he first arrived, too.

I believe that Emelina Hernandez, the maid we had in Miramar, also worked for us at the first house in Biltmore for a short time. I believe Dellis Gray joined us there after we moved in.[31] Although the address of that first house escapes me completely, I understand that Dellis Gray recently told you that it was located on Calle 197, entre 17 y 19.[32] That may be so, but I don't know for sure. I have been trying to remember the address for years with no luck. All I know is that it is the house in the picture with the four of us sitting on the front lawn that we used as a Christmas card in about 1954. In that house, the maid's quarters were built up a narrow set of stairs over the kitchen. I believe the owner was named Martinez-Fonts and I believe his first name was Alfonso, but that is all I can recall.

Our second house was at Calle 204, # 1309, entre 13 y 15, Biltmore.[33] It was a small one-story house with two bedrooms and one bath. The maid's quarters in that house were in the front off the kitchen. We had a large cistern outside the kitchen that collected rain water that was pumped to a tank on the roof where it was heated by the sun. Of course, you couldn't drink the water. We had bottled water delivered to the house. We also had a gardener named Domingo who took care of the yard and lawn. A manicurist and an ironing lady used to come to the house on a regular basis as did the milkman, eggman, and a knife sharpener among others.

The province we lived in was Havana Province which was one of six provinces. Going along the coast to the west of the Almendares River was the municipality of Marianao. Miramar, Biltmore, and other places were part of the municipality of Marianao. For some reason, out where we lived, the new developments were called "repartos" hence we lived in Reparto

Biltmore, Marianao. The Godinezes lived about a block and a half away in a house they had built with a 20 x 40 foot pool where we used to go swimming. The Nuñez and their children lived on one side of us and Rodriguez-Faura was the name of our neighbor on the other side. He had caged squirrels and other small animals in his back yard. He also had a watch dog named Titan. He was an assistant editor of some sort at the *El Mundo* newspaper where Tony Bernabei worked and he had a piece published in the newspaper to commemorate your 11th birthday party.[34,35] Rodriguez-Faura moved out shortly after the advent of Fidel Castro. I believe he moved out abruptly after the revolution and the Prairie family moved in from the Hotel Nacional where they had been staying since their arrival in Cuba shortly before Castro took over. I seem to recall Rodriguez-Faura leaving early on New Year's morning of 1959 to hide his car and his advising us to do the same.

The obstetrician who delivered your sister was Dr. Vautrin. His first name escapes me at the moment. Cindy was born in the evening - 10:50 PM on March 5, 1953. That's the same date that Stalin died in Russia. I, of course, had taken your mother to the hospital, but the details are not clear in my mind. Getting to the hospital also seems to be a blank except that I now recall that your mother's water broke at home to start things off. The doctor was called and, on his instructions, I took your mother to his office. After an examination, I took her directly to the Anglo-American Hospital. I do remember sitting in the hospital room with your mother who was in bed, but not yet ready for delivery. I recall counting contractions and the like until someone decided it was time to go to delivery. The doctor who had the duty that night was Dr. Schapelles (phonetic spelling) who had been our neighbor in our house in Miramar. I further remember that while your mother was in the delivery room, I was sitting outside the room by myself. It is true that the nurse came out of the delivery room carrying Cindy and handed her to me for a few minutes while she went about some tasks. Probably only for a few minutes. Dr. Vautrin assured me all was well. As I recall, they put Cindy in the room and a short time later your mother was brought in looking a little the worse for wear. She was knocked out by that time and not talking so I went home after a bit on advice of the doctor.

When I came back in the morning your mother was awake and holding Cindy. Cindy was banged up. Her face was bruised black and blue. Her forehead was pushed in so that her hairline met her eyebrows and then slanted back from her eyebrows to a peak on top of her head. Her eyes were bloodshot for about three weeks. Dr. Alberto De Cordoba, the pediatrician, said she would be fine as pointy-headed kids always rounded out eventually. Even though Cindy was all black and blue, I don't remember her being in danger, although she was very sick later on with chicken pox and something else. After the birth, they were both in the hospital for quite a few days, but that was customary in those days, I suppose.

Cindy was born in the Anglo-American Community Hospital. It was in Vedado, a section of Havana. It was run by the "ABC colony", a general expression used to refer to the English-speaking community - American, British, Canadian - in Cuba. The hospital was in a good sized house in what had been an elite neighborhood of big houses. It was a large house with large stone steps going up the front to the entrance and first floor. As I remember, there were three floors with an inside balcony or walkway on the second and third floors with the hospital rooms around the walkway for patients. Surgery and delivery rooms were on the third floor. There were usually several American, British, or Canadian nurses on the staff, but the doctors were Cuban many of whom were trained to a varying extent in the United States.

Shortly after Cindy was born, I went to the American Embassy and registered her birth and obtained a U.S. passport for her. All the official papers concerning her birth are in my safe deposit box.

In Cuba we attended the Methodist Church in Vedado.[36] That is where Cindy was baptized.[37] You, of course, were baptized in the First Presbyterian Church in Princeton.[38] After church on Sunday, we sometimes went passed the aquarium store as we had a tropical fish tank at home. You, of course, had your horses that you loved to ride. Your sister was too young to ride so every afternoon Dellis would dress her all in white and take her for a walk. I know Cindy says that she hated those PM walks with the scratchy petticoats. She remembers the ice-man giving her ice and getting free chocolate milk every day from the milkman. She remembers us going out one night and throwing stones at the huge land crabs and us going to the drive-in where they came out and hooked a tray onto the door of your car and served you hamburgers.

We had any number of visitors in Cuba. My father and mother came down before he died. They came over on the small passenger ship "Florida." Later, my mother came alone. At any time my mother was there, she stayed with us. That's for sure. Actually, I believe that she was there when Batista fled the country. Your Aunt Florence and Jo-Ann came down at least twice, I think, maybe more. She also came once with Ed Smith shortly after they were married. They probably stayed at a hotel I would guess even though I don't think there were any hotels in the Biltmore area. On your mother's side, her parents came down together a couple of times before your grandfather died. After that, your Grandmother Freda came down alone. Your Uncle Gene, Aunt Edith, Aunt Della, Aunt Julia and Uncle Mike, Yolanda, and Robert and Dottie also came down at one time or another. I think everyone stayed at our house, but where they all slept I don't know. Cindy says she remembers us taking your Aunt Edith out to dinner at Rancho Luna one time. Apparently, Cindy hid some chicken in your Aunt Edith's straw shell purse (the one with the flaps on top that made it look like a small picnic basket) so she could take it home to Dellis.

Other than birthdays and Cindy's birth, I can't think of any events that would have been in the newspaper.[39] Although there may have been some notice in the newspaper when my father and my brother died and when your mother's father died.[40,41,42,43,44 45,46,47,48] Of course, if we gave a party of any size, maybe once or twice a year, that was always in the newspaper, but I have no idea of any dates. Your mother and her gang had a big fund raising affair for the Havana Creche to raise money for abandoned children, but I don't know the date.[49] There is a clipping around with a picture of your mother and some others. If I find it, it may have a date. I also have some other newspaper clippings that appeared in *The Havana Post* while we lived in Cuba. One clipping is dated August 17, 1951 about our departure on the Oriente. Another is dated

September 21, 1951 about our return to Havana on the Siboney. I have another article, undated, may be about August 1956, regarding my joining the United Fruit Company. The article appeared in *The Times of Havana*. There's another clipping about our 6th wedding anniversary on January 25, 1952.

There were a number of clubs and organizations for English-speaking people living in Cuba such as the American Club, the British Club, and the Rovers Golf Club (which was British). Anyone could belong to these clubs if you applied and were accepted. There was also, of course, the Mothers' Club and the Women's Club and the Havana-Biltmore Yacht and County Club to which we belonged. You and your sister both attended Ruston Academy which was a private school owned by the Bakers.[50] Some well-to-do Cubans also sent their children to Ruston Academy which was one of two English-speaking schools in Havana where people sent their children. The other school was Lafayette. There was also a very small organization in Havana that took care of single and widowed women in a retirement/nursing home. When we first moved to Cuba and lived in Miss Ross' Boarding House for some weeks there was a single woman living there named Miss West. Apparently, she was a retired British teacher who tutored children in the English language. A few years later, she was unable to live alone and "the colony" put her in a very small nursing home. How that all worked and who paid is beyond me.

I only had two jobs in Cuba. The first was with the New York and Cuba Mail Steamship Company which was known as the Ward Line in Cuba. The Ward Line was a subsidiary of the New York and Cuba Mail Steamship Company, but the name was not used in the United States as the Ward Line owned the ill-fated passenger ship Morro Castle which was burned at sea off the Jersey Coast on a return trip from Havana in 1932 or 1933 with some loss of life. The ship was beached near Asbury Park and the burned-out hulk remained there for years. It may still be there. The press and radio had a field day with that one.

Having said all that, I can now say that I actually worked for neither of those two companies as I believe the Ward Line was non-existent in my day except on the Cuban waterfront. Actually, I worked for La Compañía Terminal Cubana Americana which was a subsidiary of the New York and Cuba Mail Steamship Company. For an American to work in Cuba, he had to be an officer of a Cuban company and be on the board of directors. At first, I was the Treasurer of the company. I was paid out of New York and my check deposited in Princeton. I paid Social Security taxes in the United States and not to the Retiro Maritima because I was an officer of the company and not covered by the Cuban retirement fund. I later became the Traffic Manager for Cuba, but stayed on the board of directors.

Later, about 1956, the New York and Cuba Mail Steamship Company sold out to a Cuban company. I was asked to stay, but I was also asked to join the United Fruit Company as the Operations Manager. I took the job and moved down the street.[51] The plan was that after a year or two breaking-in, I would become Manager of the Havana Office and all the ship operations in Cuba. The incumbent Manager of the Havana Office was to be shifted to Oriente Provence and take over the finances of the two sugar plantations and sugar mills. The problem was that by the time I was ready to take over Fidel Castro was on the loose in Oriente Province and the Office Manager's wife in Havana refused to move to Oriente. I guess she was right because in a couple of years we were all at liberty to look for a new job.

Both your mother and I spoke Spanish to some degree. Your mother spoke what the Americans called kitchen Spanish. That meant she could speak to the maids, go to the vegetable market with no trouble, talk to repair men and gas station attendants and, in general, she could get along in the city, ride the buses and so forth. I could speak a bit better as did most of the men. I could get along in the office, visit and speak to the shippers as long as I had one of the Spanish speaking cargo solicitors with me. Of course, I could get along pretty well with the longshoremen on the piers. I don't think they spoke much better Spanish than I did. What neither one of us could do was carry on a conversation with educated Cubans. On reason was that they didn't want to speak Spanish. They were all for practicing their English. The only ones of our friends who could speak Spanish well were Mel Brown and Sam Capizzi. Max Jones thought he could, but he was not very good at it.[52]

It was common talk in Havana that the Mafia was behind the spurt in hotel building to some extent at least. Most of the new hotel builders or owners were the Las Vegas crowd and they were quite well behaved in Havana. The Hollywood performers were the same as in the United States. Meyer Lansky apparently was the top dog in the Jewish-Mafia at the time. The Jews had taken over to some extent from the Italians with guys like Meyer Lansky, Dutch Schultz, and Bugsy Siegal, et. al. Incidentally, I saw Lansky walking about the casinos and glad-handing everybody any number of times. George Raft was also a manager at one hotel. Nice guy and always glad to see you. I may have mentioned it before, but I once found myself sitting beside Errol Flynn at the bar in the Hotel Nacional. We said a few words about the weather. At this time, a few movies were made in Havana. Mel Brown had a speaking role as the coroner who examined a dead body. I saw it on TV once. The Godinezes and a couple of other people we knew were extras in a movie filmed in one of the casinos. They walked around and said "Oh, here she comes now."

As I recall, Batista held elections in late 1958 and his puppet (Rivero Aguero) was elected. He became President-elect and lived at the corner of our street. After the election, guards were always on duty outside his house. This was good in a way as no one could enter our street from either end without being checked out by the Army. We just drove past and waved.

I mention this because your mother and I went to the Brown's house for a New Year's Eve party on December 31, 1958, and on the way home as we entered our street there were no police or Army guards, no people, and no lights in or around the President-elect's house. What was wrong? We had no idea. At the other end of our street, where an Admiral lived, there were no guards and no lights either. We were so dumb it never occurred to us that Batista and his cohorts flew the coop. In any case, that was the end of the Mafia in Cuba.

As I recall, my mother was visiting us when Batista took a powder. I don't think your other grandmother was there at that time. Of course, I am not sure of any of these events. There was no marshal law after Batista left. In fact, there was no law. Some of the police department was around to keep order and you may remember that the students from Villanova University were active and around with their armbands sporting some date or another. They were stopping cars on the main street passing the school and looked for guns. No one was really in charge for the first week or so. It took Castro a week or so to come up from Oriente Province with the barbudos who began to set up guard posts and restore some order. I think your Grandmother Freda came down a bit later, but I am not sure. The first year or so a provisional government was set up by Castro and he appointed all kinds of good guys to run the various Cabinet positions and so forth. Everyone wanted to give Castro a chance, etc. Of course, all the bad guys were shot after a fair two-hour trial.

We left Cuba in mid-March, 1960.[53,54,55] I have no idea any more where we stayed for the last few weeks before we left Cuba. In fact, I hardly remember the place other than it was a two bedroom furnished apartment close to our house in Biltmore. I think it was in the La Playa area. We flew Pan American Airlines to Miami and then National Airlines to Philadelphia. No one knew we were coming.

All our possessions were left on the United Fruit Company pier in Cuba. Our household goods arrived in the United States on the S.S. Arctic Gull V9 on August 17, 1960, at the Port of New York, North River.[56] They arrived on the last United Fruit Company ship to sail from Havana before the company was taken over by the Cuban Revolutionary Government. The two lift vans containing our belongings were not on the cargo manifest and it created a minor problem with U.S. Customs when the United Fruit Company tried to deliver them to us in Princeton, so I had to go in to New York to explain what it was all about. The man in Havana who ordered our furniture loaded on the Arctic Gull was named Pepe. He was President of the Longshoreman's local that covered the section of the waterfront which took in the Ward Line and the United Fruit Company. I knew him as he worked as a pier foreman for the Ward Line. If it weren't for Pepe, we probably never would have received any of our things.

LIFE AFTER CUBA

After we left Cuba in March 1960, we lived briefly with my mother at 1606 S. 53rd Street in Philadelphia where we temporarily enrolled you and your sister in Mitchell grammar school so that you could finish out the school year. During the summer of 1960, we moved to Princeton, New Jersey, where we lived with your other grandmother at 630 Princeton-Kingston Road. In September, after our furniture arrived from Cuba, we moved to a rented house on Clover Lane in Princeton.

The fall after we returned from Cuba was really the first exposure you and Cindy had with a heavy leaf fall. You both played in the leaves in front of your grandmother's house in Princeton. You used to bury Cindy completely in leaves. Also, that heavy leaf fall was followed by a very heavy pre-Christmas snow fall which was the first snow that either of you had ever been able to play in. Later, in the winter of 1961, Cindy came down with scarlet fever and you had pneumonia. She was quarantined at home at the same time that you were in the hospital.

The summer of 1961, we built a house at 11 Colonial Avenue in Princeton Junction, New Jersey. We sold the house in 1985 when I was transferred to Norfolk, Virginia. We actually lived across the river from Norfolk in the town of Portsmouth where we rented a townhouse at 105 Crawford Parkway. The house faced the Elizabeth River so your mother and I could watch the port operations from our bedroom balcony on the second floor of the house. That is where your mother died on August 28, 1987, from chronic lymphocytic leukemia.[57,58] I stayed on in Portsmouth until I retired in 1992. After that, I moved to Plantation, Florida, where I live at 325 N.W. 95th Avenue.

I joined the Amerind Shipping Corporation in May 1960 as Operations Manager. Amerind was owned by the Hans Isbransen family who were fairly large ship owners and operators in New York. Amerind was a pier and terminal operator and general agent for European and South American companies who owned and operated cargo ships and tankers. For much of the same period, I was also the General Manager for Ship and Terminal Operations for U.S. Bulk Carriers, a subsidiary of Amerind. U.S. Bulk Carriers operated 15 American ships under charter to the United States government in support of the Vietnam War effort. These positions entailed extensive travel to the Middle-East, India, Japan, Vietnam, etc., including a one-month business trip (with your mother) around the world in 1966. We left New York for Japan in mid-September and returned, via Rome, in October. You were away at college at the time and Cindy stayed at home with both your grandmothers.

I left Amerind in April 1967 to pursue a career as a Marine Transportation Consultant with Coverdale and Colpitts. For nine months in 1968, I was assigned to Kuala Lumpur, Malaysia. Your mother and Cindy accompanied me during that stay. That was the first trip around the world for your sister and the second for your mother. I later returned to Malaysia for a three month study of the Island and Port of Penang. Then, I made a number of other maritime studies before leaving that position in June 1970. After that, I was engaged briefly by Amerind Container Services, Inc., as General Manager - Operations to supervise operation of seven container ships.

In August 1971, I joined the Maritime Administration Eastern Region Headquarters in New York City where I served as Port and Inter-modal Development Officer. The waterfront was changing rapidly in those days. As a result, one of our principal concerns was facilitating the evolution of east coast ports and port facilities so that they could load and unload ships carrying cargo to and from foreign ports in large (40 by 8 foot) containers weighing between 30 and 40 tons each. During this time, I was also an alternate member of the New England River Basin Commission. It didn't mean much, but we did produce a fairly comprehensive report on New England ports and facilities which was well received and we put out five reports concerning the transfer of containers from ships to railcars (and vice versa) at five east coast ports.

In January 1978, I was appointed Ship Operations Officer. My responsibilities in this job included administration of Eastern Region activities relating to ship operations and ship repair including all the government-owned training ships that were on loan to the state maritime colleges in Maine, Massachusetts, and New York. We also operated training facilities in New York and New Jersey such as the Radar and Fire Fighting Schools where ships officers received up-grade training and re-certification required by the U.S. Coast Guard.

At some point, the Maritime Administration was transferred from the Department of Commerce to the Department of Transportation. And, in 1980, the Maritime Administration Eastern Region began to reorganize itself to support the newly established Ready Reserve Fleet (RRF) with the objective of creating and maintaining some thirty ships in such a reserve state that they could be activated and fully crewed for service within 5 to 10 days.

During this time, a bit of a power struggle developed between the Eastern, Western, and Central (Gulf) Regions and the Office of Ship Operations in Washington, D.C. I was temporarily assigned as Deputy Director of the Eastern Region from August 1980 to January 1982. Then I was appointed Ship Operation Officer. My office was in New York, but I reported to the Office of Ship Operations in Washington, D.C.

I was transferred to Norfolk, Virginia, in September 1985 to become Chief of the Division of East Coast Ship Operations, a newly created entity. At first, the division consisted of a National Defense Reserve Fleet anchored in the James River off Fort Eustis with about 120 employees, the office in Norfolk with 3 or 4 marine engineers/surveyors and supporting clerical staff, and a ship operations office in New York. We immediately began to augment the engineering staff to about 20 professionals over a two year period. The new division was part of the Office of Ship Operations in Washington, D.C., and it was responsible for all Maritime Administration ship operation activities on the east coast of the United States.

In October 1987, the Division of East Coast Operations was abolished and the South Atlantic Region was established with me as Director reporting directly to the Maritime Administrator. We continued with all of our ship operations and training functions, but our big emphasis was on developing the Ready Reserve Fleet (RRF) to a level of about 30 ships. We were quite successful in this effort which was proven when most of the fleet was activated for the transport of equipment and supplies in support of the U.S. armed forces during Operation Desert Storm (also known as the Gulf War) which began in January 1991. I retired in 1992 after almost 22 years with the Maritime Administration. They capped my career with a big retirement party - dinner dance and cruise on the Elizabeth River. As you know, it was well attended.

———————————————

NOTES TO: My Chambers Family, An Oral History

1.   The original Certificate of Baptism for Mary Ann McCauley dated January 20, 1893, at the Tabor Presbyterian Church, 18th and Christian Streets, was in the possession of William Scott

Chambers, 325 N.W. 95th Avenue, Plantation, Florida 33324.

2.   A card concerning the mid-air collision is in the possession of Thomas Wallace Chambers' daughter, Jo-Ann Chambers Smith Skinner, 1268 New Bedford Lane, Reston, VA 20194. The card says that S/Sgt. Thomas W. Chambers qualified as a member of the Caterpillar Club on July 8, 1944, his life having been saved in an emergency jump by use of parachute equipment. Awarded by the Irving Air Chute Company.

3.   The original Marriage Certificate and Wedding Booklet for Mary Ann McCauley and Henry G. Chambers was in the possession of William Scott Chambers, 325 N.W. 95th Avenue, Plantation, Florida 33324. The Wedding Booklet indicates that the marriage was performed by Freeman Bovard, Pastor of the First Methodist Episcopal Church. The names of the wedding party are indicated as Mrs. Frederick Queroli, Mr. John Smith, and Mrs. Freeman Bovard.

4.   According to William Scott Chambers, his mother had previously been engaged to a man named Ed Hentges and his father had previously been engaged to a woman named Florence Keidel.

5.   The details of Henry G. Chambers' service in the U.S. Navy during World War I were confirmed by the National Personnel Records Center, Navy Reference Branch, 9700 Page Avenue, St. Louis, Missouri 63132-5100. For reference purposes, Henry G. Chambers' World War I service number was 1210254. A copy of his service record is in the possession of his granddaughter, Kathryn C. Torpey, 5035 Domain Place, Alexandria, Virginia 22311-5066.

6.   According to William Scott Chambers, his mother may have received a World War I widows pension (XC 178-12-712) for a brief period after which she was told that she was not eligible.

7.   Letter dated September 20, 1999, from Kaye Thomas, Director of Administrative Services, Masonic Home of New Jersey, 902 Jacksonville Road, Burlington, New Jersey 08016-3896 states that the Grand Lodge record indicates that Henry Grafe Chambers became a Master Mason on March 16, 1943, and died November 10 (sic), 1953.

8.   Letter dated December 30, 1999, from Anita R. Erickson, Right Worthy Grand Secretary, Grand Chapter, Order of the Eastern Star of New Jersey, 111 Finderme Avenue, Bridgewater, New Jersey 08807-3101 indicates that Mary Ann Chambers was initiated on March 7, 1944, into Camden Chapter # 35.

9.   Letter dated January 24, 1997, from Bill Poulos, Director of Public Affairs, Railroad Retirement Board, 844 North Rush Street, Chicago, Illinois 60611-2092 transmits a copy of the claim folder for Henry Grafe Chambers, SSN 717-09-5980, and states that because he died while still working in the rail industry, his records contain less information than would those of someone who actually retired on the basis of age and service. Also, as only survivor benefits were paid to his widow, Mary Ann (McCauley) Chambers, WD273038, there is no information in the file pertaining to railroad service performed by Henry Grafe Chambers prior to 1937.

10.   News Story and Photograph, *The Evening Bulletin*, Friday, July 18, 1947, p. B (New Jersey Edition). This news story, entitled "Smoke Control Unit Proposed in Camden," states that Henry G. Chambers, an engineer-foreman for the Pennsylvania-Reading-Seashore Lines, was an attendee at a meeting held by the Public Affairs Commissioner concerning a proposal to curb industrial smog in Camden.

11.   The picture of the Kingsessing Recreation Center basketball team is in the possession of Kathryn C. Torpey, 5035 Domain Place, Alexandria, Virginia 22311-5066.

12.   The Sunday School medals belonging to Thomas W. Chambers were in the possession of his brother, William Scott Chambers, 325 N.W. 95th Avenue, Plantation, Florida 33324.

13.   The original Certificate of Baptism for William Scott Chambers dated April 10, 1921, at the Tabor Presbyterian Church was in the possession of William Scott Chambers, 325 N.W. 95th Avenue, Plantation, Florida 33324.

14.   A picture of the Tom Thumb wedding was in the possession of William Scott Chambers, 325 N.W. 95th Avenue, Plantation, Florida 33324.

15.   According to the Admission Book of the Pennsylvania Nautical School (1896-1947), FHL Microfilm Roll 1018399, William Scott Chambers (# 2689) was admitted to Class # 40 on October 18, 1939, and graduated on October 24, 1941.

16.   The details of William Scott Chambers' service in the U.S. Merchant Marine are contained in his service record at the National Maritime Center, U.S. Coast Guard, 4200 Wilson Boulevard, Suite 510, Arlington, Virginia 22203-1804. A copy was also in the possession of William Scott Chambers, 325 N.W. 95th Avenue, Plantation, Florida 33324.

17.   According to Robert M. Browning, Jr., *U.S. Merchant Vessel War Casualties of World War II*, (Annapolis, Maryland: Naval Institute Press, 1996), pp. 118-122, the following U.S. merchant ships were lost on Convoy PQ-16 due to enemy action: **CARLTON (5/24/42); SYROS, 2 dead, (5/26/42); ALAMAR (5/27/42); ALCOA BANNER (5/27/42), CITY OF JOLIET (5/27/42); and MORMACSUL, 3 dead, (5/27/42).**

18.   According to Robert M. Browning, Jr., *U.S. Merchant Vessel War Casualties of World War II*, (Annapolis, Maryland: Naval Institute Press, 1996), p. 132, the **S.S. STEELWORKER** struck a mine while the ship was moving to her anchorage in Kola Inlet, Murmansk, USSR, after having discharged 375 tons of ammunition. The authorities in Murmansk theorized that an enemy airplane had dropped the mine, it had become embedded in mud, and worked loose.

19.   According to Robert M. Browning, Jr., *U.S. Merchant Vessel War Casualties of World War II*, (Annapolis, Maryland: Naval Institute Press, 1996), p. 152, a mine struck the **S.S. ALCOA CADET** while she lay at anchorage at Kola Inlet, Murmansk, USSR. The authorities at Murmansk speculated that an enemy mine had been dropped in the harbor by aircraft and had eventually worked loose, surfaced, and struck the ship.

20.   According to Robert M. Browning, Jr., *U.S. Merchant Vessel War Casualties of World War II*, (Annapolis, Maryland: Naval Institute Press, 1996), pp. 172-175, the following U.S. merchant ships were lost on the "ill-fated" Convoy QP-13 when the vessels mistakenly steamed into an Allied minefield near Iceland because of the convoy commodore's inability to get a good navigational fix due to poor visibility and foul weather (fog): **RICHARD HENRY LEE (7/5/42); MASSMAR, 48 dead, (7/5/42); HYBERT (7/5/42); JOHN RANDOLPH, 5 dead, (7/5/42); and HEFFRON, 1 dead, (7/5/42).**

21.   Two of the black elephants with ivory tusks were in the possession of William Scott Chambers, 325 N.W. 95th Avenue, Plantation, Florida 33324. The third black elephant was in the possession of Dellis Gray, Calle Cuba, # 507, entre Teniente Rey y Muralla, Habana Vieja, Cuba.

22.   The U.S. Merchant Marine World War II service medals (including the Russian commemorative medal) were in the possession of William Scott Chambers, 325 N.W. 95th Avenue, Plantation, Florida 33324.

23.   William S. Chambers Collection, (AFC/2001/001/18182), Veterans History Project, American Folklife Center, Library of Congress includes an 18-page document containing a brief description of the voyages he made from October 1939 to September 1946; the names of the ships, the owners, and the capacity in which he served on the ship; and a description of the cargo carried and the method of loading and discharge of the cargo. The document was written by William S. Chambers in 1949 while he was attending the Massachusetts Institute of Technology.

24.   According to a letter dated February 21, 1945, from Kathryn Judith Freda to her sister, Gloria A. Freda, the latter was living at 202-09 43rd Avenue, Bayside, Long Island, New York. The letter is in the possession of Kathryn C. Torpey, 5035 Domain Place, Alexandria, Virginia 22311-5066.

25.   Birth Certificate for Kathryn Judith Chambers, March 26, 1947, volume 23, page 288, # 4985, Division of Vital Statistics, Boston, Massachusetts.

26.   The original Birth Certificate for Cynthia Scott Chambers, March 5, 1953, is in the possession of Cynthia Scott Chambers, 1450 S.W. 70th Avenue, Plantation, Florida 33317.

27.   The following news stories concerning our arrival in Cuba appeared in the newspaper:

News Story, *The Havana Post*, Tuesday, December 19, 1950, p. 5.

OFF THE GANGPLANK

Arrivals from New York today on the "Siboney", of the Ward Line, are Mr. and Mrs. Edwin Randall, Dr. and Mrs. Americo Grimaldi, Mr. and Mrs. William Chambers and son (sic); Dr. and Mrs. Joseph Salerno.

News Story, *The Havana Post*, Saturday, December 23, 1950, p. 5.

OFF THE GANGPLANK

W. S. Chambers came in as passenger from New York to Havana on the
"Siboney" of the Ward Line, this past Tuesday. He is to be in for some time for
the Cuban American Terminal Co. Douglas Singer is the president of the firm.

28.   Shipping News - Departures, *New York Times*, Saturday, December 16, 1950, p. 29 says
that the Siboney departed on December 15, 1955, for Havana. Apparently, the Siboney, which
belonged to the Cuba Mail Company (aka Ward Line), sailed from Spring Street in New York
City and carried mail and parcel post for Cuba as well as passengers and cargo.

29.   Daisy (Ricketts) Gonzalez's daughter, Estela "Cha Cha" (Gonzalez) Brown Barry
provided information regarding her mother's relationship to my mother. Estela was a
pharmacist. She was retired from the Food & Drug Administration. She had a son named
Manuel Serge Brown and a grandson named Juan Miguel Brown. She died June 23, 2013. At
the time of her death, she was married to David Barry of 5750 Bou Ave # 1011, Rockville,
Maryland 20852-5632, (301) 881-9328. Her obituary was published in *The Washington Post* on
July 7, 2013. It read as follows:

ESTELLA (sic) A. BARRY (Age 84)

A resident of Rockville, MD, departed this life on June 23, 2013. Estella (sic)
was a beloved wife, mother, grandmother, and friend and will be greatly missed.
She is survived by her husband, David Barry; one son, Manuel S. Brown;
grandson, Juan X. Brown; and a large extended international family. Memorial
Services will be held on Wednesday, July 10, 2013 at 10 a.m. at St. Elizabeth
Catholic Church, 917 Montrose Rd., Rockville, MD 20852.

30.   In an e-mail dated July 22, 2000, Estela (Gonzalez) Barry, 1714 Evelyn Drive, Rockville,
Maryland, 20852-4127, said that her maternal grandparents were John and Lillian Ricketts.
Lillian Ricketts was born in Grand Cayman and moved to Cayman Brac where her three children
were born. Her husband, John Ricketts, worked for an American shipping firm. At that time, the
Caymanians worked mainly as seamen. John Ricketts was offered the opportunity to move to the
United States since his company sailed out of Mobile, Alabama. John Ricketts liked the idea of
living in the United States and accepted the offer, but Lillian Ricketts refused to come to live in
the South of the United States. She knew about racism in the United States and was not
interested in living under those conditions.

John Ricketts took his son, Chesman, to Mobile where he enrolled him in a boarding
school in Alabama. After that, Lillian Ricketts moved to Cuba with her two daughters (Daisy
Ricketts who was about 7 years of age and her older sister, Minna Ricketts, who was about 9).
Many years later, Chesman Ricketts decided to come to Cuba where he stayed with his mother,
Lillian Ricketts. Estela is not sure in what year her Uncle Chesman got the job with the
Caribbean Sugar Company at Central Macareño in Camaguey, but Estela says that her

grandmother, Lillian Ricketts, used to go almost every year to Central Macareño to visit her son, Chesman. Estela would accompany her grandmother on these trips to Camaguey. She loved it. They would ride the train. The countryside was beautiful. That is where Estela met Dellis Gray. Years later, the Administrator at Central Macareño, Samuel Meigs, retired and Estela's Uncle Chesman moved to Daytona Beach, Florida, with the Meigs family.

Meanwhile, in Havana, Estela's mother, Daisy Ricketts, married Luis Manuel Gonzalez, a musician, who was born in Camaguey. He played the trumpet in the big bands in Cuba (theater musicals, dances, and casinos including an exclusive nightclub called Sans Souci and the Tropicana Nightclub in Havana). Their daughter, Estela, was confirmed at the Iglesia del Espiritu Santo and had her first communion at the Iglesia de Nuestra Senora de la Merced, both historic Catholic Churches in Habana Vieja.

Daisy (Ricketts) Gonzalez was the chef and manager of Miss Carolyn Ross' Boarding House in Vedado. Miss Ross always relied on Estela's mother to hire (and sometimes fire) workers. The boarding house was very well known for its food among foreign diplomats and business people (American, British, Canadian, Dutch). Based on its reputation, Ernest Hemingway (and maybe his wife) came to be a guest at the boarding house. It was there that Estela's mother cooked for Ernest Hemingway. He was particularly fond of a curry dish that Estela's mother prepared especially for him.

While Estela doesn't know exactly when her mother arranged with Dellis Gray to go to work for my parents, she knows that her mother had met my mother years before when we stayed at the boarding house. It seems that Estela's mother came in contact with many people while she worked at the boarding house, so she was always helping people find workers or she was helping find jobs for people who needed to work.

Daisy (Ricketts) Gonzalez also worked for Carmen and Joseph Butler (Esso Standard Oil of New Jersey) while they lived in the suburban section of Havana then known as Country Club. After the Revolution, Daisy (Ricketts) Gonzalez and her husband, Luis Manuel Gonzalez, left their residence on Calle Jesus Maria, # 117, entre Damas y Cuba, Habana Vieja, on June 6, 1959. They eventually settled in Washington, D.C., where their daughter, Estela (Gonzalez) Barry, had lived since 1952. Daisy (Ricketts) Gonzalez died in 1986. Her obituary appeared in *The Washington Post* on December 4, 1986. It read as follows:

> DAISY GONZALEZ 79, a native of Cuba who moved to the Washington area in 1965 and became active in church organizations, died of a heart ailment Nov. 24 at George Washington University Hospital. She lived in Washington.
>
> Mrs. Gonzalez was a past member of the council of the Catholic Church of the Nativity in Washington where she also was a member of the Solidarity and Sacred Heart League. As part of her work on the parish Eucharistic Committee, she had made infant baptismal gowns and stoles.
>
> She helped plan and organize the first meal program for the Hispanic Senior Citizens

organization here.

Before coming to this country, she operated a boarding house in Havana that catered to American and British diplomatic clients. Diners at her establishment, which was known for its curry dishes, included the writer Ernest Hemingway. She came to this country in 1960 and lived in New York City before coming here.

Survivors include her husband, Luis M. Gonzalez of Washington; one daughter, Estela Barry. and one sister, Minna Ricketts, both of Rockville; one brother, James Rankin of Puerto Limon, Costa Rica, and one grandchild.

Her husband, Luis Manuel Gonzales died on March 7, 2001. His obituary was published in *The Washington Post* on March 10, 2001. It read as follows:

LUIS MANUEL GONZALEZ - MUSICIAN

Luis Manuel Gonzalez, 96, a Cuban-born trumpeter who was featured in Havana nightclubs in the 1940s and '50s and who performed with Latin bands in the Washington area from the 1960s to the '80s, died of pneumonia March 7 at the Hebrew Home in Rockville. He had a heart ailment.

He played with the Victor Aponte Orchestra and in clubs, at the American Folklife series at the Library of Congress and for dances and galas at hotels that included the Hotel Washington and Shoreham Americana. Mr. Gonzalez, who was profiled in The Washington Post at the end of 1999, was a native of the coastal city of Camaguey, where his father ran a music academy. He moved in 1937 to Havana, where he started playing in private clubs and cabarets. He left for New York in 1959, during a period of increasing economic hardship in Cuba, and moved to Washington in the early 1960s.

Mr. Gonzalez was a member of the Catholic Church of the Nativity in Washington and the Musicians Union. His wife, Daisy Gonzalez, died in 1986. Survivors include his daughters, Estela Barry of Rockville and Zoila Alpizar of Hyattsville; two grandsons and a great-grandson.

Estela's grandfather, John Ricketts died December 11, 1950 in Mobile, Alabama. Her grandmother, Lillian L. Ricketts died on May 7, 1965 in Washington, D.C. Her obituary was published in *The Evening Star* on Saturday, May 8, 1965. John Chesman Ricketts died in Bethesda, Montgomery County, Maryland, on February 19, 1960. His obituary was published in *The Evening Star* on Tuesday, February 23, 1960. Minna G. Ricketts died on February 25, 1988.

31.   In a conversation with Dellis Gray on June 11, 2000, at her quarters in Old Havana, (Calle Cuba, # 507, entre Teniente Rey y Muralla, Habana Vieja, Cuba), she told me that she was born in Camaguey, Cuba, on June 6, 1929. Her parents were born in Jamaica. Her father's name was Ivan Gray Gaynor and he was from St. James. Her mother's name was Beatrice Hemmings and she was from Westmoreland. Her parents arrived in Camaguey around 1919 when her father was nineteen and her mother was seventeen. According to Dellis Gray, it was her uncle, Herbert Hemmings, who brought her mother to Camaguey after his World War I service. Apparently, there are many people of Jamaican descent in Camaguey.

Dellis said that in Camaguey she first worked for Mr. and Mrs. Meigs at Central Macareño. Mr. Meigs was with the Caribbean Sugar Company. It was at Central Macareño that Dellis met Chesman Ricketts, the brother of Daisy (Ricketts) Gonzalez as Chesman also worked for Mr. Meigs. Later, Dellis came to Havana where she worked for my parents while my father was with the United Fruit Company.

32.	Dellis Gray believes that the address of our first house was Calle 197 entre 17 y 19, Biltmore. She cannot remember the house number, but said it was across the street from the house belonging to the Entrealgos who owned the El Encanto department store located at Galiano and San Rafael. That the owners of the El Encanto department store lived across the street from us was confirmed by my father, William Scott Chambers, who said that they had provided for their housekeeper in her old age by having her stay on with them. Apparently, in retirement, she was in the habit of sitting on their front porch every day for hours at a time.

33.	Regarding our second house in Biltmore, Dellis Gray said that our neighbor to the right as you faced the house was Enrique Rodriguez-Faura (who was the social editor for a newspaper in Havana known as *El Mundo*). His wife was named Lulu and their housekeeper was named Dalia. Although my diary (January - December 1959) indicates that Rodriguez-Faura moved out on January 15, 1959, and the Prairie family moved in on January 16, 1959, Dellis said that Rodriguez-Faura may still live in that house.

On the other side was Raul Nuñez and his wife, Estrudes Mestre. Apparently, the Mestre family owned Radio-Television CMQ. Dellis says that Mrs. Nuñez was critical of my mother for allowing Dellis to enter and exit our house via the front door. Apparently this just wasn't done. Dellis says that my mother said, "I trust her with my daughters, so she can come and go by the front door." Dellis also said that on Tuesdays my mother would get a list from her of what she wanted to eat and would go to the store and buy it including rice, beans, plantains, and bistec (beef). Dellis claimed that Mrs. Nuñez disapproved of this, too, and is reported to have said that the maids should eat picadillo and soup made from whatever the family was eating.

Other neighbors included Julio Iglesias de la Torre who owned the estate on the corner across the street from us. He was with the Shell Oil Company. The house was quite large and the grounds contained a playground and a zoo. At the end of the block was a house belonging to Rivero Aguero, Batista's puppet and the president-elect of Cuba. At the other end of the block, was the house belonging to José M. Rodríguez Hernández, a Comodoro in the Cuban Navy. Dellis said that Dionisio San Román was tortured and assassinated in that house in the early morning of December 12, 1957 for crimes he allegedly committed in an uprising in Cienfuegos against the government of Batista. Dellis further said that his body was later thrown into the sea.

Around the block from us was the house belonging to the Godinez family. They were good friends of my parents. Dellis said that Batista's son, Papu Batista, lived next door to the Godinez family and that he had a large swimming pool. She also said that Batista's daughter was married to the son of Perez Benitoa who lived three blocks away from us and was in the habit of arriving home in a helicopter. Dellis' recollections could not be verified. Her reference to

Batista's son may be to Ruben who attended Princeton University in New Jersey and had his suits made by my grandfather, Guerino Freda. My grandmother once told me that Batista's son offered to transport items to Cuba for delivery to my parents whenever he was taking a trip home.

34.   News Story, *El Mundo*, (Havana, Cuba) Viernes [Friday], 28 de Marzo de 1958, p. B-8.

Comida

Los estimados esposos William Chambers y Gloria de Chambers, ofrecerán una comida mañana en su residencia del Biltmore, para agasajar a su hija, la encantadora niña July (sic) Chambers, que arriba a sus once años de edad.

Del simpático acto participará un selecto grupo de amiguitas de la festejada.

35.   News Story and Photograph, *El Mundo*, (Havana, Cuba) Viernes [Friday], 4 de Abril de 1958, p. B-2.

UNA COMIDA DE niñas, que resultó alegre y animada en extremo, se celebró en días pasados en le residencia que en el reparto Biltmore poseen el señor William Chambers y señora Gloria de Chambers, estimado matrimonio de la colonia norteamericana.

Con el infantil ágape festejaron a la mayor de sus hijas, la linda y encantadora Judy Chambers, que cumplía los once años de edad, disfrutando de la grata reunión un corto grupo de amigas de la adorable festejada.

En la fotografía que publicamos, aparece Judy, en compañía de Caroline Berstene, Carol Dallas, Jeanne McDonald, Melissa Wubbold y Jane Potts. (Foto L. Marrero).

36.   According to Peter E. Carr, *Guide to Cuban Genealogical Research - Records and Sources*, (Chicago, Illinois: Adams Press, 1991), p. 28, the Methodist Church in the Vedado Section of Havana was founded in 1883. Dellis Gray told me that the church is located at Calle 25 and K in Vedado. When I went to see the church, I noticed that the building has a plaque on it which says July 21, 1950. Dellis told me that she attended this same church while we lived in Cuba as she is a Methodist. I remember that we attended English-language services in the morning. She said that she attended services in the evening.

37.   The original Certificate of Baptism for Cynthia Scott Chambers, dated December 20, 1953, at the Cathedral Methodist Church, Vedado Section, Havana, Cuba, is in the possession of Cynthia Scott Chambers, 1450 S.W. 70th Avenue, Plantation, Florida 33317. The baptism was performed by the Reverend Charles P. Schulhafer.

38.   The original Certificate of Baptism for Kathryn Judith Chambers dated June 29, 1947, at the First Presbyterian Church, Princeton, New Jersey, is in the possession of Kathryn C.Torpey, 5035 Domain Place, Alexandria, Virginia 22311-5066.

39.   News Story, *The Havana Post*, Friday, March 13, 1953, p. 8.

SOCIETY

Mr. and Mrs. William Chambers
Announce Birth of Baby Girl

Mr. and Mrs. William S. Chambers announce the birth of a baby girl born March at the Anglo-American Hospital.

Mr. Chambers is an official of the Cuban American Terminal Company (Ward Line).

40.   In addition to a news story that is said to have appeared in *The Havana Post* on Friday, November 13, 1953, (this edition of the newspaper is missing from the microfilm reel at the Library of Congress), the following obituary appeared in the *Camden Courier Post*, Wednesday, November 11, 1953, p. 4, concerning the death of Henry G. Chambers:

H.G. Chambers
Is Dead at 56

Harry G. Chambers, 56, of 21 Wayne Gardens Apartments, Collingswood, road foreman of engines for the Pennsylvania Reading Seashore Lines, died suddenly Tuesday (sic) night at his home.

A native of Philadelphia, Mr. Chambers resided in the Camden area for 13 years. He joined the railroad as a fireman in 1916, was named engineer in 1926, Assistant Foreman in 1942, and Foreman in 1945.

Mr. Chambers was active in Masonic groups. He was a member of Camden Lodge 15, FAM; Tall Cedars of Lebanon, Forest 5; Cyrene Commandery and Siloan Chapter 9, RAM. He was also a member of the Brotherhood of Locomotive Engineers.

Surviving are his widow, Mary, two sons, Capt. Thomas W. Chambers, serving with the Army in Korea, and William Scott Chambers, of Havana, Cuba; two grandchildren, and his mother, Mrs. Josephine Chambers, of Philadelphia. Services will be held at 11:00 AM Monday in the Murray Funeral Home, 408 Cooper Street, where friends may call Sunday night.

41.   Thomas Wallace Chambers was killed in the crash of a jet trainer-bomber on October 6, 1955, at Shaw Air Force Base in Sumter, South Carolina.

42.   News Story, *The Havana Post*, Sunday, October 9, 1955, p. 6.

William Scott Chambers, traffic manager with the Ward Line, went to Columbia, S.C. the night of Friday and by plane, once he was informed his brother, an officer in active service for the Air Force in the States, and (sic) [had] met with death by accident. Friends and officials and fellow workers with him in the

43.	News stories concerning the death of Thomas W. Chambers appeared in the following South Carolina newspapers:

News Story and Photograph, *The State: South Carolina's Progressive Newspaper*, (Columbia, South Carolina) Saturday, October 8, 1955, p. unk.

News Story, *Sumter Daily*, (Sumter, South Carolina), Friday, October 7, 1955, p. 1.

44.	News stories concerning the death of Thomas W. Chambers appeared in the following Philadelphia newspapers:

News Story, *Philadelphia Inquirer*, Friday, October 7, 1955, page 1.

News Story and Photograph, *The Evening Bulletin*, Friday, October 7, 1955, page 29.

The news story and photograph that appeared in *The Evening Bulletin* read as follows:

2 Area Fliers Killed in South

West Phila. Captain, Birdsboro Youth Die

Shaw Air Force Base, S.C. Oct 7 - Two fliers from the Philadelphia area were killed in the crash of a jet trainer-bomber here last night.

The dead were Captain Thomas W. Chambers, 32, son of Mrs. Mary Anne (sic) Chambers, of 1606 S. 53rd St. and Airman Second Class John Volpiccini, 20, of 103 River Road, Birdsboro.

The plane, an RB57B, was of the type used for photographic reconnaissance. It was on a routine training flight when fell in a wooded area and burned.

A veteran of 12 years' service, Captain Chambers served in Europe during World War II and later in Korea. He was graduated from John Bartrum High School and New Jersey State Teachers College, Glassboro.

Captain Chambers formerly lived in Collingswood, New Jersey. Surviving, besides his mother, are his wife, the former Florence Clark, of Merchantville, and their three month old daughter, Joan (sic).

Volpiccini was graduated from Birdsboro High School where he played soccer and baseball. He was nearly halfway through a four year enlistment.

He is survived by his mother, Mary; four sisters, Mary, Palma, Mrs. Angelina Testa and Mrs. Bernette Smail, and three brothers, Frank, Anthony, and Nicholas.

45.   The following letter concerning the death of Thomas W. Chambers was in the possession of his brother, William Scott Chambers, 325 N.W. 95th Avenue, Plantation Florida 33324:

43rd Tactical Reconnaissance Squadron (NF)
Shaw Air Force Base, South Carolina
14 October 1955

Mrs. Mary A. Chambers
1606 S. 53rd St.
Philadelphia, Pennsylvania

Dear Mrs. Chambers,

It is with deepest regret and sympathy that I write you on this occasion.

I have been your son's Commanding Officer for the past six months, and knowing Tom as I did, I believe I can understand how you must feel at his death.

Before Tom was assigned to this squadron, he was working in the Maintenance Squadron. He wanted to come down here and several of the airmen that had known him and worked for him ask me if we could get him.

This is unusual as you may guess, for it is not often that airmen think so much of an officer that they ask for him by name. It was not long before I could understand it, for there was something special about Tom. He was not always easy with the airmen, but he knew what was to be done, and he did it with the full support of everyone that worked for him.

Tom had a young officer working for him that was trying hard to do a good job, but did not know how to handle the airmen. I used to tell this young officer, "Watch how Tom handles the airmen in any given situation and you will learn a lot ". He had almost a hundred airmen working for him and every one of them loved him.

A couple of months ago, our Base Commander realized that he had to do something to increase the maintenance capability of the base. He established a school and nicknamed it "Tool Box". He needed a good officer to run this school. Your son was selected over all the other maintenance officers on the base and I know that it was a wise choice for I knew how Tom worked.

Mrs. Chambers, even though I had only known Tom for about six months, I could go on and on telling you about his outstanding achievements here. He has been an exemplary officer, he has been known and loved by so many many people and contributed a great service to the United States Air Force and to this great country of ours.

As Chaplain Combs said at the memorial services held for Tom, "Captain Chambers is not dead and will never die in our hearts and minds - he has only left us for a while".

Mrs. Chambers, there is little I can tell you about the accident until the board has finished its investigation, but I can tell you that Tom was not at fault. When these things happen with no apparent reason, it makes us realize that there is still a God that controls our destinies.

We here in the 43rd Tactical Reconnaissance Squadron were busily getting ready for a maneuver or exercise called "Sagebrush" and Tom was helping to get the aircraft ready. Tom and some of his men were working late to test fly one of the B-57's. The flight was uneventful until a few minutes before landing they crashed not far from the base. The boy that was with him was Airman Volpiccini. " Volp", as we called him, was an excellent crew chief and very devoted to Tom. As I wrote to Mrs. Volpiccini, "If Volp knew that his airplane was going to crash with Tom he would still have gone along, he was that conscientious about his work and devoted to the man he worked for".

Mrs. Chambers, I have been flying for thirteen years and have lost some of my best friends through accidents. It is dangerous work, but none of them have hit me as hard as this one. It is a great loss to you, to us who had also learned to love Tom and to the country he served, but I hope you will find strength in the fact that he lived a good life and that he contributed much to his country. Your son was a good pilot, a fine officer and a Christian man.

It is possible that with the information we have as a result of this accident and the salvaged airplane, we can learn enough to prevent recurrence. I am sure that if Tom knew that he had also contributed to this in making the airplane safer and saved other lives, he would indeed rest in peace.

We here in the 43rd Tactical Reconnaissance Squadron wanted you to know that we loved Tom and that you have our deepest sympathy. We pray that God will give you strength to bear this for you can certainly be proud of the way he lived and we will all have his memory.

Sincerely,

PAUL C. VANDERHOEK
Major, USAF
Commander

46.   Obituaries concerning the death of Thomas W. Chambers appeared in the following Philadelphia newspapers:

Obituary, *Philadelphia Inquirer*, Wednesday, October 12, 1955, page 46.

Obituary, *The Evening Bulletin*, Wednesday, October 12, 1955, page 25.

The obituary that appeared in *The Evening Bulletin* read as follows:

CHAMBERS - On Oct 6, 1955, CAPT. THOMAS W., husband of Florence Clark Chambers, of 1606 S. 53rd st., Phila., aged 32 years. Funeral services Friday, 11 A.M., at the Murray Funeral Home, 408 Cooper st., Camden, N.J. Friends may call Thursday evening.

47.   According to an undated note (ca. November 17, 1996) from Dennis Cangiarella, Vice-President, Locustwood Memorial Park, Route 70 W, Cherry Hill, New Jersey 08002, Thomas Wallace Chambers was buried in that cemetery in October, 1955 in Section 2, Lot 425. His headstone reads as follows:

Thomas W. Chambers
South Carolina
Capt 43 TAC Recon SQ AF
World War II Korea AM & OLC
March 25, 1923 October 6 1955

48.   News Story, *The Havana Post*, Sunday, July 24, 1955, p. 3.

Colony Column

SINCEREST SYMPATHY to Mrs. William S. Chambers whose father passed
away at his home in Princeton. Mrs. Chambers is expected to return on the
weekend from Princeton as she was present at the funeral...

49.   News Story, *The Havana Post*, Sunday, October 11, 1953, p 3. This news story, entitled
"Creche Habana Nueva To Hold Benefit Party Wednesday", said that Mrs. William Chambers
was a member of an Auxiliary Committee holding a benefit card party on Wednesday to raise
funds for the Creche Habana Nueva.

50.   In 1950, Ruston Academy was located at Calle G esq. 5a in Vedado. In the fall of 1956,
Ruston Academy moved to a new location at Calle 190, # 2102, entre 21 y 23, in Alturas del
Country Club, Marianao.

51.   News Story, *The Havana Post*, Wednesday, August 1, 1956, p. 5.

William Chambers Joins
Staff of United Fruit

The local offices of the United Fruit Company announced today that William S.
Chambers, formerly Assistant to Vice President of the local Ward Line
organization, will join the staff of the United Fruit Company in the capacity of
Assistant to the Manager of the Havana steamship agency. Chambers will
assume his new position with the United Fruit Company on or about August 15,
1956.

Chambers was born in Philadelphia, Pa., on February 25, 1921. He married the
former Gloria A. Freda and they have two daughters, Scynthia (sic) and Judith.

Chambers has been steamship Captain with the United States Lines, is a graduate
of the Massachusetts Institute of Technology with the Degree of Bachelor of
Science in Marine Transportation. He is also a marine engineer and has served
in the capacity of Assistant Port Captain for the Ward Line on their New York
piers.

Chambers came to Cuba in the capacity of Treasurer of the local Ward Line
organization and during the past two years has been associated principally with
their traffic department.

52.   Photograph, *The American Club Bulletin*, No. 167, April 30, 1960, Havana, Cuba, p 3, contains a photograph of my parents with their best friends. The caption reads as follows:

> ST. PATRICK'S BUFFET - Club members celebrating St. Patrick's Day at the March buffet are Sam Capizzi and Jean Brown in the center foreground and seated clock-wise, Gloria Chambers, Charles K. Miller, Elaine Capizzi, Bill Chambers, Jane Daugherty, Mel Brown, Joyce Miller, and Earl Daugherty.

53.   Dellis asked me if I remembered when the ship named La Coubre blew up in Havana Harbor on March 4, 1960. Although I have no recollection of this happening, Dellis said that she and my mother were very afraid for me because they didn't know where I was at the time. The ship in question was a French freighter carrying Belgian armaments for Cuba. When the ship exploded, it killed more than 80 Cubans. Fidel Castro blamed the CIA. During the funeral ceremonies, Castro coined the new phrase, "Patria o Muerte," which is still in use today. The atmosphere was tense. Counter-revolutionary groups became active. In the midst of the gathering chaos, my father said he asked the United Fruit Company to relocate my mother, my sister, and me to Florida. They didn't think it was necessary. In their view, Castro was nothing more than another petty dictator who could be dealt with in time. My parents disagreed, so they obtained our exit permits and my father had our belongings packed and moved to the United Fruit Company docks. Then, according to my father's memory, we left Cuba by plane on March 30 (sic), 1960 (his grandparents' wedding anniversary date). Dellis Gray said that on our last day in Cuba, we all got into the car, dropped her off at her cousin's house on Calle 29, entre 42 y 44 in the Almendares Section of Havana, and left for the airport. I have no idea what became of the car.

54.   The VIGENCIA (exit permit) from the Republica de Cuba, Ministro de Defensa Nacional, Departamento Tecnico de Investigationes de la Policia National Revolucionaria, dated March 7, 1960, for Kathryn Judith Chambers is in the possession of Kathryn C. Torpey, 5035 Domain Place, Alexandria, Virginia 22311-5066.

55.   The following e-mail dated February 2, 2011, from Jane (Spraggins) Daugherty Wilson to Kathryn C. Torpey, says we left Cuba on March 24, 1960.

> Hi Kay,
>
> I wrote in my appointment book that I went to the airport on March 24, a Thursday to see Gloria off. It seems to me that she left with you and Cynthia and that Bill left later or was it earlier. I looked through my book and did not find any entry for seeing Bill off. Could it be that he went back by ship? I think I stayed until sometime in July.
>
> Also, I wrote that there was a dinner party for Bill and Gloria at Jean [Brown]'s on March 12; on March 18 we had lunch at the Biltmore and bridge at Joyce Miller's for Gloria. On March 19, we all had dinner at Sue Godinez's home for Bill and Gloria. It was the custom to entertain when people left Cuba. Unfortunately, I stayed too long and did not get to be "feted" because all my friends and Goodyear people were gone. I can't remember what we gave Gloria as a going away gift but she gave all of us a set of pottery mugs (without handles) that were made in Cuba. I still have mine. On second thought, I think I gave her a pair of gold stud earrings. I can't remember

what they were called but traditionally, Cuban women wore them to bed at night and the name reflected that.

If I can help in remembering Cuban days, I will be happy to try.

Jane

56.   The Arrival Notice of Possessions from Cuba (Household Goods and Personal Possessions), dated August 17, 1960, was in the possession of William Scott Chambers, 325 N.W. 95th Avenue, Plantation, Florida 33324.

57.   Death Certificate for Gloria Freda Chambers, August 28, 1987, # 00860 & 87-029423, Division of Vital Records, Richmond, Virginia.

58.   A memorial service was held for Gloria (Freda) Chambers in Princeton, New Jersey, on Saturday, September 12, 1987. The funeral home was filled to capacity. Many of those attending the memorial service had known her since she was a child. Following the memorial service, two of her long-time friends, Jack and Cindy Servis, invited everyone to their house. Gloria (Freda) Chambers was buried in a private ceremony on Monday, September 14, 1987, in Princeton Cemetery, in the Freda family plot, Lot 19, Section 2, Map 3.

Obituaries concerning the death of Gloria (Freda) Chambers appeared in the following New Jersey newspapers:

Obituary, *Princeton Packet*, (Princeton, New Jersey) Friday, September 11, 1987, p. 8B.

Obituary, *Town Topics*, (Princeton, New Jersey) Wednesday, September 9, 1987, p 25.

Obituary, *Trenton Times*, (Trenton, New Jersey) Wednesday, September 9, 1987, p D6.

The obituary that appeared in the *Trenton Times* read as follows:

Gloria Freda Chambers

Portsmouth, Virginia - Gloria Freda Chambers, 66, died August 28 of leukemia at Maryview Hospital, Portsmouth, Virginia.

Mrs. Chambers was a long-time resident of the Princeton area before moving to Portsmouth two years ago.

She was a retired employee from United Jersey Bank.

Surviving are her husband, William S. Chambers; two daughters, Kathryn C. Hogan-Torpey of Alexandria, Virginia and Cynthia Chambers Rosenbaum of Plantation, Florida; her mother, Filomena Q. Freda of Princeton; a brother, Eugene G. Freda of Trenton; and two grandchildren, Allison and Marissa Rosenbaum, both the Plantation, Florida.

A memorial service will be held at 11:00 AM Saturday at the Kimble Funeral Home, 1 Hamilton Avenue, Princeton, with the Reverend Cynthia Ann Jarvis, associate pastor of the Nassau Presbyterian Church, Princeton, officiating.

Burial will be private. Friends may call Saturday from 10:00 AM until time of service at the funeral home.

Index to Appendix B

Index to Appendix B

INDEX

INDEX

114

INDEX